FRIENDS OF THE LIBRARY

An Interactive Novel

by Nathan A. Haverstock

CREATIVE PEOPLES PRESS

OBERLIN, OHIO

ISBN: 0-7880-2126-5
LCN: 200410701

Designed and Illustrated by John Swiers

First Edition

Printed in Lima, Ohio

FOR THOSE WHO CHERISH PUBLIC LIBRARIES

-- and especially Zachary Clemens Freed, Eleanor Bolan
Freed, Zoey Sheldon Poll, Jonah Sayre Freed, Eliza Catherine
Haverstock, and Nathan Robert Haverstock - exemplary
readers and grandchildren.

To the Reader

If you have never taken pleasure in letting your fingers play along the tops of the cards in a burnished hardwood catalogue tray, never felt the warm glow of a lamp in the main reading room of a public library, nor experienced the ecstasy of discovery in such a place - you are probably well advised to look elsewhere than this book for amusement.

For herein is a tale told to delight and alarm those who cherish libraries even as they do their spouses and most intimate companions. The author's hope is that it may afford people who love books and magazines a final opportunity to bathe in the clear, deep and fast running stream of nostalgia, while awaiting a day that will not return unless they, like the friends of the Plymouth Public Library, do something about it.

The town of Plymouth is an invention, though it is similar to several wonderful small settlements in northeast Ohio, like the one where the author lives. There day in and day out, the public library makes available the sum total of mankind's knowledge free of charge to anyone who crosses its threshold. Any resemblance of the characters in this book to real people, living or dead, is wholly accidental.

Contents

Chapter 1

TEN DOLLARS

There were noticeably more people than usual on the broad stone steps waiting for the Plymouth Public Library to open on that Saturday in early March, 1998, thanks to an unprepossessing-looking man in their midst.

Unbeknown to those around him, he had invested ten one-dollar bills in carrying out a half-baked scheme of his own devising, which would lead to a revolution in local library patronage of staggering proportions and a revival of reading -- feats that may be duplicated anywhere there is a friend of a library like him, lucky enough to have a copy of this book.

The gentleman in question, to give him a name, was Hawley Short, an entirely average sort of person in his late sixties, with a moon face, a thick mane of gray hair, and a highly intelligent wife, who was devoted to curbing his enthusiasms. This is his story, the tale of a rare triumph of altruism in an age of cynicism and avarice.

It had begun in the previous week when Hawley, acting on impulse, had randomly hidden the aforementioned dollar bills in the pages of ten books newly acquired by the library. His objective, as he said later to his wife, was simply to promote reading, though he also confessed to a certain boyish curiosity to see what would happen. He was motivated, too, by a feeling he shared with many people of his age around the country - a deepening despair over the fate of books and the unsettling changes that had overtaken libraries during recent years.

He believed that the dictionary's definition of libraries as "repositories of knowledge," was anachronistic, that they had become -- as anybody with a brain in his or her head knew -- librarians foremost among them -- chiefly centers for entertainment. Beginning with the youngest patrons, children, whose special preserves within most libraries had become miniature

1

"theme" parks devoted to reinforcing consumption demands generated by Disney and Hollywood.

Moving up in age, were the latchkey youngsters, for whom libraries had become places to hang out after school and socialize, as noisily as possible (as it seemed to older patrons), while waiting for their parents to get home from work.

Worst of all, as Hawley Short believed, public libraries had become so complicated to use, thanks to all the new gadgets, that they had lost, as down some Orwellian memory hole, their former principal virtue -- the ease with which people of all ages, classes and conditions could obtain access to their treasures. The elderly and the underprivileged, he lamented, were often hopelessly intimidated by all the machinery called into play simply to borrow a book, and unable on fixed incomes to afford the mechanical contrivances needed to operate what libraries increasingly lend -- videos and compact disks.

With the approach of the millennium, Hawley was filled with a disheartening premonition -- that the sort of library he had grown to love over his ifetime was about to lapse suddenly and irreversibly into historical obsolescence. The craft of the librarian, he feared, like that of the carriage maker, would soon be relegated to museums, and books themselves become artifacts of a lost culture.

But Hawley, like a lot of otherwise ordinary people, was not to be defeated easily or without a fight. He believed that "One Person Can Make a Difference," which was the motto of the college in the town where he lived. Like other residents of Plymouth, a community of a few thousand souls set on the flatlands of northeast Ohio, he also had an abiding faith in the Almighty. "Only in Plymouth," people often said, when something happened that was unexpectedly timely or thoughtful -- like the local plumber dropping in for a chat at the precise moment the sink overflowed, for example, or an anonymous donor supplying the cash the soccer team needed to buy new jerseys -- acts of good fortune or kindness that still occurred regularly in small towns of Ohio.

Drawing on that faith, plus his innate good cheer and a certain puckish sense of humor, Hawley had decided to take some small action on matters that were dear to his heart, as they must be to all those who, like him, are friends of libraries. Such people, he had concluded, could no longer sit

2

idly by or cover their eyes in the face of what was happening.

So much for Hawley's nobler impulses. In carrying them out, as he had only loosely inserted the dollars where they could be readily found next to the title page, seven were discovered within a couple of days. Their lucky finders had told family and friends, and in the process, multiplied the value of Hawley's original investment through exaggeration. Single dollars had become tens or twenties in the retelling, a sum of sufficient size in the aggregate that the <u>Plymouth Gazette</u> -- a weekly "Noise-paper," as Hawley generically called all such rags -- had run a little feature on an inside page of Friday's edition, headlined "$$$$$ FOUND IN LIBRARY BOOKS."

"Looks like we're onto something," he bubbled effusively to his wife, when he called her attention to this gratifying acknowledgment of his action before bounding out the door that Saturday morning, headed for the monthly meeting of the Council of the Friends of the library. Arriving a little early he was jubilant to see that the story in the <u>Gazette</u> had attracted some new faces to the library. There were also people he recognized, waiting on the stone steps, who hadn't set foot in the library in years.

"There is nothing like the prospect of getting something for nothing to bring out the good people of Plymouth," he mumbled to himself with smug satisfaction as the clock on the town hall struck nine, and Eric Motley, a kindly-looking old gentleman, nodded in his direction, before unlocking the tall, heavy wooden doors from inside. Whereupon the library, like a vacuum cleaner, sucked all those milling about in the cold outside into its warm inner chambers where the sum total of human knowledge was available daily free of charge, even on Sunday after church.

Thereafter, Motley, who was a relic of a long-gone era, when the library's main reading room was a place for peaceful reflection and thought, polished and put on his spectacles before assuming his accustomed place behind the reference desk on a chair worn smooth by his many years of faithful service. He was then ready, like those of his honorable calling around the nation, to assist patrons with diligence and good cheer, no matter how arcane or outrageous their requests.

That morning Braxton Augustus, a small but resolute young African-American boy wearing a worn jacket that was missing a couple of buttons, was first in line. He wanted help in reading what he called "some old newspapers," for reasons that Motley was too discreet to inquire about, in

3

keeping with the high ethical standards of his profession.

Meantime, in a hallway off to one side of the reading room, which led to a small conference room, a beaming Hawley Short was soon joined by the other members of the Council, all of whom were chattering like magpies about the story in the <u>Gazette</u>.

"Greed be with you!" he exulted, as he approached these, his dearly beloved comrades -- "The True Believers," as he had long ago christened the stout hearts who faithfully showed up once a month to discuss how they might be helpful to the troubled institution, which was the focus of their common affection.

But his words were lost in the din, above which he heard the high-pitched voice of the librarian, Louella Winters: "We don't know who put the money in the books or how much, but there were no tens or twenties" she exclaimed! "So far as we know, the <u>Gazette</u> just made that up out of thin air."

Her declaration elicited another burst of animated conversation. And it was not for some little time, until calm was fully restored, an assortment of mugs set out on the table where coffee was brewing, and the members of the Council had sat down in their chairs, that Hawley could get a word in edgewise.

"For the record," he said authoritatively, casting his eyes knowingly around the group, "the total amount of money put in books at this library was just ten, I repeat, just ten, one-dollar bills!"

"How can you be so sure of that?" asked Charles Whitney, a tall and balding local banker. His friendship for libraries had begun when he was sustained spiritually and intellectually by the books delivered by gray ladies on the same carts that delivered his meals and medicine during the nearly two years he had spent recovering at a veterans hospital from the severe wounds he had received in Vietnam.

"Because I put them there!" Hawley declared, triumphantly. "I did it!" "But why?" asked Lydia McGovern, an ageless lady of slight proportions but a determined will. She made her way about town in all seasons on a bicycle, the necessities of her simple life strapped on the back in a faded carpet bag -- a box of herbal tea, a sketch pad, a thin but closely-woven sweater, and a tightly-sealed can of lubricating oil."To promote reading," Hawley said."Wonderful!" exclaimed Lydia. "What a good idea! I think I'll do the same thing."

But Neal Barker, an aggressively, upwardly-mobile African-American of about thirty-five years of age, who made his living selling computers and software, was less enthusiastic. Barker was often the odd-man out at Council meetings. He delighted in pulling the tails of those around the table, who were among his dearest friends, reminding them that after all was said and done the Plymouth library was merely an historical period piece, a repository of mostly Honky culture, en route to the globalization of information through the internet.

"This miracle," as his preacher father might have said in a Sunday sermon, was placed here on earth in accord with the Almighty's plan, the younger Barker believed, finally and definitively to level the playing field in a world where most people are emphatically not white.

"You would have done better to hide the money in a compact disk, a CD ROM," Barker said, "or under the keyboard of the computerized card catalogue we'll soon be installing."

"Can't do it all by myself," snorted Hawley, "have to leave something for the rest of you."

"If that's a challenge, I except it gladly," said Barker. Then, scarcely aware of what he was committing himself to, he reached across the table and shook hands with Hawley, sealing a wager that would have far-reaching implications for all the members of the Council who, despite whatever difference might momentarily divide them, were drawn together by their common, deep and abiding bond of affection for the library.

Drawing on this reservoir of good will, the nattily dressed Preston Myers, a stockbroker who had campaigned vigorously for the post of chair of the Council as a means of advertising his services within the community, smiled approvingly.

"Then we're all in this together," he said, looking around the table, as everybody nodded.

"The decision is unanimous, then!" added Louella Winters, who made a note of it, little reckoning on the enormous consequences that would in time flow from their action that day, as they sat around a much-scarred table and drank abominably bad coffee from cracked mugs, with fake, powdered cream and a syrupy sweetener.

It fell to María Álvarez, at twenty-five years of age the youngest member

5

of the group, to have the last word on the matter. Before speaking, she pushed up her glasses on a nose so thin it might have belonged to one of Modigliani's models, thus magnifying her large, auburn eyes.

"I think that what Hawley did was wonderful," she said in a charming contralto, before leaning around the end of the table and planting a kiss on his cheek amid a ripple of laughter all around, as the meeting broke up.

"I think it's wonderful that you are going to do something, too, Neal," she said, but Neal was on his feet before she could decorate his cheek in similar fashion.

Chapter 2

Hawley's Nightmare

"What's that? How much did I put in books and why?" Hawley Short said, repeating aloud the question asked by a cub reporter from <u>The Plain Dealer</u> in Cleveland, who had gotten his number from Louella Winters and called a couple of weeks later. The reporter, on a slow day for news and badgered by his editor to come up with a feature, had spotted the story in the <u>Gazette</u>, and thought it might be worth a follow-up.

"It was just ten one-dollar bills," Hawley affirmed, "and I am happy to set the record straight after the exaggerated account in the <u>Gazette</u>.

"Now, as to why I did it, it's a bit more complicated. To be honest, I did it just to see what would happen.

"In retrospect, I must say it seems in keeping with our times, a logical way to focus people's attention on reading in an age when getting something for nothing has become the national rage. It's no secret, for example, that our authorities here in Ohio raise money for our schools through lotteries, the results of which you dutifully run on your second page. Even as we speak our governor is proposing that we combine our lottery with those of other states to swell the size of the pot.

"He's not the only one pandering to the public's enthusiasm for games of chance. Today's publishers, for example, are selling subscriptions to magazines of constantly deteriorating literary merit by promising to enter a new subscriber's name in a sweepstake -- the grand prize a swell Caribbean cruise for two. Purveyors of candy bars of diminishing size are making chocoholics inspect the backs of sticky wrappers on the odd chance they won a million dollars. Our federal immigration authorities now determine those who will become eligible for U.S. citizenship among the great unwashed masses of foreign lands through drawings.

"And as for the folks who were here first -- the Indians -- look at the way our government has figured out to help them get ahead -- by granting 'em licenses to open gambling casinos on their tribal lands. So that at last they can scalp us -- and legally, too, with our elected leaders providing the axe.

"Why, the extent to which we have already converted this land of opportunity into a gamble-ocracy, is evident to the most casual reader of your newspaper, or any newspaper, for that matter. All that's lacking is a series of good strong editorials by one of your most talented wordsmiths, supporting the replacement of the bald eagle with a pair of dice. You could make a persuasive case, too, I think, for issuing postage stamps with the faces of smiling jackpot winners or some of the high-rollers on Wall Street, who have stolen blind their shareholders and become today's folk heroes.

"But don't get me started," Hawley continued, suddenly realizing that, as usual, he was talking too much. "To tell you the truth I am somewhat fatigued from an afternoon spent raking last year's leaves off some promising-looking daffodil tendrils.

"What am I going to do next?" he said, slowly repeating aloud the reporter's final question for the benefit of his wife, who was listening intently to his end of the conversation.

"Well, I don't rightly know. I'm a little tuckered out at the moment. But I can tell you this much: I've been forking it over, you might say. By the way, the other members of the Council of the Friends of the Plymouth Library are, too. We're all in this together, trying to think up ways to promote reading - and computer literacy, too, whatever that is. They'll be coming up with some dynamite ideas, you'll see.

"Meantime, for myself I am figuring out how to make it a little harder for people next time, maybe hide some dollars in books in the stacks that are well worth reading, but which haven't been checked out for a long time. That might help save them from being discarded or pulped. At any rate I understand that all ten of the dollar bills I originally planted have been discovered.

"Maybe I'll up the ante a little. But I'm here to tell you we're not rich, me and the Missus, just friends of the library, people who like to read books, that sort of thing. And if some of your readers are as concerned as we are about the future of reading in Ohio and America, tell 'em we'd appreciate it if they went down to their libraries and did the same thing, invest a few dollars of their own."

"Do you suppose someone will?" Mrs. Short asked after her husband had hung up, outraged that the reporter had called so late -- at nearly nine thirty.

"You never know," Hawley replied, stifling a yawn. "This is a great nation. People often sort of bumble along until someone -- in this case, if I may say so, yours truly -- raises a flag to say 'whoa, enough already.' Then there's no stoppin' 'em, Americans, I mean, regular folks, like you and me."

Hawley yawned deeply as the cat nestled on his wife's lap, and he reiterated feelings they both deeply shared. "Libraries used to be such simple places, my dear, so easy to use. They were places where the downtrodden masses could get a leg up on life. People like our María Álvarez, for example, the only daughter of migrant Mexican farm laborers, who came up here to Ohio to pick cucumbers and tomatoes for the Vlasic Pickle and Campbell Soup folks about a hundred miles west of here.

"She was practically in tears once, when she told me about why she had first visited a library out west of here, where to Ohio's disgrace migrant Chicanos still live like serfs while harvesting something for us to eat. She wanted to wash her hands and face, she said, after a sizzling hot day in the fields. On leaving the ladies room she was amazed to learn that she could actually have her very own temporary library card, borrow books and a few old magazines in Spanish to read out at the camp.

"Neal Barker, too. He told me he practically got his education at the library, the public high school was so bad in the Black neighborhood where he grew up in Mississippi.

"Never happen nowadays.

"Libraries have become so dang-blasted complicated, you practically need a degree in engineering just to check out a book.

"I remember not so many years ago at meetings of the Friends Council, we talked about improving the lighting in the reading room, repairing the catalogue trays, budgeting more for heat so that we could keep longer hours during the cold, dark months of winter -- when reading is such a special joy! -- raising funds for a new wing to provide space for more stacks and more books. Those were subjects we could all, myself included, understand. Now all we seem to talk about are mechanical gadgets that

9

we really don't know anything about. Like at our last meeting, you'll never guess, my sweet pea, what we talked about?"

A quizzical expression lit up his wife's deeply lined but beautiful face, as she softly asked: "What?"

"A fax machine, that's what, and when it came to a vote there was the usual line-up, yours truly in the minority along with the two other regular Luddites, Lydia and María -- three votes to four. Predictably, one of the four was Neal Barker, whom I can always forgive because after all machines are his stock in trade. Incidentally, he told me he makes a bundle selling 'em to the local college, which will buy anything billed as the latest, no matter how expensive. According to Neal that's why colleges around the nation have to keep on raising their tuition faster than the rate of inflation.

"Then there was pompous Preston Myers. He can always be counted upon to vote for anything advertised as leading to greater efficiency. But I was sort of surprised when banker Charles Whitney, who always has his eyes firmly fixed on our bottom line, went along. Not nearly as surprised, though, when Louella Winters did. She told me once in strictest confidence that any librarian who resists automation nowadays runs the risk of being labeled old-fashioned and given the gate."

Having delivered himself of sentiments familiar to his wife, as to anyone who knew him, Hawley headed upstairs to bed, where he soon fell into a deep sleep despite having brought along one of his favorite books. In his dreams he was transported to the days of his boyhood when libraries consisted of helpful people, an alphabetical card catalogue, and books. The more books and the more people checking them out, the better the library, the prouder the librarian. It was a simple equation.

Besides telephones and typewriters, which were located out back where members of the staff worked in utopian tranquillity, the only apparatus commonly found in libraries back then was the microfilm reader. There was no denying that it saved an enormous amount of space previously taken up in storing bulky and smelly old newspapers. In time it had become possible to subscribe to the newspapers themselves on microfilm, which had resulted in saving money spent on subscribing to them in bulk via the mails.

Though space had to be set aside for the device on which the film was read -- a somewhat larger table than the standard library reading carrel --

the microfilm reader was -- and remains to this day -- the only machine still in use in libraries across America, which has paid for itself.

The same most emphatically could not be said of the next mechanical intruder in Hawley's nocturnal survey of things past. This was the copying machine, where people have been systematically breaking the spines and bindings of books virtually since the day of its introduction, and on which the federal government in Washington had insisted that a notice be posted in an absolutely futile attempt to enforce the nation's copyright laws.

Besides threatening the health of books and consuming prime space, the early copier was a noisy contraption. There was the constant jingling, as patrons deposited coins in a receptacle that was forever jamming up. Moreover, the machine -- a harbinger of those to follow -- had soon created the need for additional machines. These included the troublesome one which changed only the most pristine of dollars bills, fresh from the mint, into quarters, dimes and nickels to feed the copier's insatiable appetite, as people -- even reputable scholars -- gave up taking notes entirely, in favor of the faster and more reliable copying of pages, chapters, even whole books -- to take home, where they could read and mark them up at their leisure.

This was not to mention all the hours spent by members of the library's staff in collecting, counting, and rolling up all the quarters, dimes and nickels -- with some librarians insisting that a second person be present to insure the honesty of the tabulation. Nor the need for employees of the library to learn to operate all the buttons on the increasingly complex control panels of the quirky devils and clear up paper jams, which were of frequent occurrence. Nor the constantly escalating costs of leasing a copier. Nor the endless, unanswered calls to the repair people supplied by its maker, who were the only ones who could fix it when anything other than the most rudimentary problem occurred. Nor the way the number of these wizards declined exponentially, as the copier population underwent an explosion.

The next mechanical intruder on the library scene, speaking chronologically, was the electric typewriter. No sooner was this indispensable handmaiden of progress and efficiency in place, than it was difficult to obtain the ribbons and eraser tapes without which it was so much dumb junk. Again, there were all the hours expended in teaching

11

the library staff how to use it before, like successive generations of electric typewriters, it became obsolete. This became known when repair people sent out by corporate America wrung their hands in despair over the "old" models, even as they handed out brochures on the new models whose ribbons, as they hastened to point out, were in plentiful supply.

By then, of course, the noisy old copying machine, capable of making only black and white copies of a predetermined size, was itself obsolete. It was replaced by newer, and ever more costly models with marvelous new features. These were brought to the market one at a time so as to enhance sales to libraries whose patrons were now demanding them. Copying machines that could collate the pages of a report, were followed by ones that could enlarge and reduce page size for patrons willing to learn the ever more intricate details of how to operate them. These were followed by copiers which could reproduce pages in a few colors and then in many colors, and print on both sides of the same piece of paper.

By this juncture it was incumbent upon libraries to hold special classes on the increasingly arcane operations of the machines for staff and patrons alike. The libraries were thus transformed -- without audible complaint -- into sort of vocational training schools for the corporations that manufactured and sold the machines.

By then, as one generation of machines followed another, the new copiers would no longer accept coins, but demanded a card. The machines that had changed dollar bills into coins were replaced by machines, which accepted only the most crisp one-dollar and five-dollar bills (and to people's frustration rejected those that were rumpled or worn), and entered the value of those that passed muster on a plastic card. The wallets and pocketbooks of library patrons perforce had to accommodate this card in addition to their regular library card, which was itself soon to sport a sticker with a personal, machine-sensitive I.D., or bar code, without which it was impossible to charge out a book.

But that, as Hawley twisted and turned in his bed -- his dream become a familiar nightmare -- had been only the beginning. For onto the scene had marched the word processors at which most members of the library staff now seemed to stare all day long to the detriment of their vision and self-esteem. These machines, not incidentally, had in the span of a few years utterly destroyed the familiar ambience of libraries. Beautiful maple and oak tables, crafted to read books on, were drilled with holes to accommodate all the cords and cables needed to power them.

Moreover, the word processors themselves, quite apart from relegating the electric typewriters to obsolescence, required months, not just days or weeks, to learn to operate. Once libraries had become dependent upon them, corporate America soon came up with generations and generations of ever more costly and complicated accessories, called "software."

And all the while, as the mechanical side of operating a library became more and more intricate, what librarians had learned in earning their degrees in graduate school might as well have been written upon the water for all the good it did them. It was of no more use to them in the practice of their profession than learning to manipulate the gossamer craft the Wright Brothers flew at Kittyhawk to the pilot of a modern jet aircraft.

This is to say nothing of the inequities and anxieties suffered by befuddled librarians whose salaries were -- and are! -- but a pittance, as compared with those of the makers and purveyors of hardware and software.

The subjugation of the Plymouth library to the Satanic power of Bill Gates and his ilk was soon to climax in a sort of pre-millennium grand finale with the installation of a computerized catalogue. This would effectively relegate to the scrap heap of history the sum total of librarianship, going back to the founding of the great library at Alexandria, Egypt, three centuries before Christ.

At the Plymouth library, this grand tradition was embodied in the beautifully crafted catalogue trays which had cards alphabetically arranged within three categories, author, title and subject, and embellished with cross-references bespeaking a high order of human intelligence. These were soon to be replaced by cold keys and a so-called "word processor," which as Hawley would soon learn in buying one for himself, incorporated idiotic games and a category called "Browse," in a craven appeal to hopeless dilettantes

The old card catalogue would be removed from the Plymouth library, and an accumulated storehouse of knowledge representing more than a century of careful nurturing, scattered to the winds at some land-fill "without a tear! Without even a decent burial!" Hawley exclaimed aloud, as he awoke from his nightmare with a start, and heard his wife saying: "Hawley, you're having that dream again."

"You're right, my tootle-ootle, you're right. But never again, and remind me to tell you why not in the morning, because with Neal Barker's help you and I are going to surrender to the winning side."

While the Shorts slept, the reporter from The Plain Dealer finished his story, and sent it along through a sleepy copy editor to the make-up man. The latter, himself a regular patron of a local library, cut some nonsense out of a story from Washington to make room for it in a special box on the front page.

Thus it was that before Hawley had even made coffee or fed the cat that Sunday morning, people all around the Cleveland metropolitan area were reading "PLYMOUTH MAN HIDES DOLLARS IN LIBRARY BOOKS."

"In the hope that other people who want to promote reading will act on his example," the article began, "Hawley Short of Plymouth put ten one-dollar bills in books recently acquired by the local public library two weeks ago.

"Reached by phone last night, Short said that all of the dollars have been discovered, that he is mulling over doing more of the same, maybe even putting bills of larger denominations in books, and making them harder to find. He emphasized, however, that he is not a rich man, and called upon friends of libraries everywhere to help him promote a revival of reading, and wean the younger generations from the boob tube.

"Plymouth librarian Louella Winters confirmed that Short belongs to the Council of the Friends of the library. She said that the other members of the Council had unanimously endorsed Short's action soon after they heard about it. Moreover, individually and collectively they are contemplating additional initiatives in a similar vein to promote not only reading, but also computer literacy.

"Since Short planted money in books, patronage at the Plymouth library has increased markedly, according to Winters. 'The idea that you just might find a dollar in one of our books seems to appeal to people,' she said.

"'Many of the new patrons, who were attracted by the publicity in our local paper about the dollar bills, have checked out books, too,' she added. 'It seems they had sort of forgotten that's what we have in the library. And you know we have had nearly one hundred requests for new library cards. All of which makes us extremely happy.'"

14

Chapter 3

S TREET PERSON

In the days following the front page story in <u>The Plain Dealer</u>, residents of northeast Ohio showed once again, true to form, how quickly they can respond to a worthwhile idea, like cleaning up Lake Erie and stocking it with walleye. Or building a new baseball stadium for the Cleveland Indians. Or in deciding to renovate the ornate old downtown public library building instead of bulldozing it, as people would have done in a lot of other places.

While gratified by the show of support for his initiative, Hawley Short was not surprised. The Buckeye State, as he was enormously proud of reminding whomever would listen, buys more books per capita than any other state in the U.S.A., including such paragons of intellectual prowess as Massachusetts and New York.

In keeping with this devotion to the printed word, newspapers all around Ohio were soon reporting a blizzard of discoveries of money in books. Some of the mostly anonymous copycats acted for reasons of local chauvinism. Ohioans living in the vicinity of the birthplaces of seven U.S. Presidents, for example, took it upon themselves to dollar-ize books by and about their native sons who had served in the White House.

"And a dangerous place for them, too -- the White House, I mean," said Hawley to his wife, "considering that two Ohio-born Presidents, Garfield and McKinley, were assassinated, and a third, Harding, was poisoned by his wife, if you believe the conspiracy theorists.

"But isn't this nice?" he said, calling her attention to an item about how the first Presidential library established in the United States, which is located near President Rutherford B. Hayes's home in Fremont, was offering a prize -- to be conferred upon the student writing the best essay based on the materials in the library's collections.

"A golden opportunity for some imaginative youngster to unravel why Hayes, of all people, became involved in arbitrating rival claims by three South American nations -- Argentina, Bolivia, and Paraguay -- to the jungles and swamps of the Gran Chaco region, when he was in President in 1878," Short noted, "if you will forgive me a little show of pedantry. The Paraguayans were sufficiently pleased with his efforts that they named one of their country's largest departments Presidente Hayes.

"It's got to be a funny story, how a place came to be named after someone who had never set foot there, or for that matter anywhere in the South American continent. There is at least an inch of cards about it waiting to be explored in the Hayes library."

As befitting a state that stamps its license plates with the legend "BIRTHPLACE OF AVIATION," dollars aplenty were found in books all over Ohio, which chronicled the history of flight. In Dayton youngsters, who checked out admiring biographies of the brothers Wilbur and Orville Wright, discovered coupons good for banana splits at a local ice cream shop. In Columbus a flight school hid coupons in books on local aviation legend Eddie Rickenbaker. They entitled their finders to free trips of a half-hour's duration aboard a vintage Ford Tri-Motor airplane.

Newspaper stories about discoveries of rewards in works on local heroes proved prelude to a statewide trivia craze on local radio and television stations, as Ohio headed toward the celebration of its bicentennial in 2003. There were awards of theater tickets or dinner for two for correctly identifying the hometowns of astronauts John Glenn of Cambridge, the first American to orbit the earth in a space capsule; and Neil Armstrong of Wapakoneta, the first earthling to leave his footprint on the moon; inventors Thomas Alva Edison of Milan; and Charles Martin Hall of Oberlin, who discovered the process to make aluminum; and movie stars Tyrone Power and Roy Rogers -- both from Cincinnati -- Clark Gable of Cadiz, Paul Newman of Cleveland, and Dean Martin of Steubenville.

The lucky respondent to one radio call-in show won the grand prize of a thousand dollars for coming up with the name of the first Ohio resident to serve as the Librarian of Congress -- custodian of America's national library in Washington, D.C. The correct answer was Ainsworth Rand Spofford, who was living in Cincinnati when President Abraham Lincoln named him to the post in 1864 -- partly as a reward for a flattering biography Spofford had written of the 16th President.

Another caller, who identified herself as a library reference specialist, won a dinner cruise for two on Lake Erie for correctly identifying the director of the Cleveland Public Library who served in that post. The answer was L. Quincy Mumford, who was appointed by President Eisenhower -- "and the only Librarian of Congress up to that date who had a degree in library science," the caller noted.

Youngsters in Canton, Ohio, home of Pro Football's Hall of Fame, were delighted to find much sought-after cards celebrating gridiron stars, in worshipful biographies of sports heroes at the local library. In Gilmore, a tiny settlement about five miles south of Gnadenhutten as the crow flies, the local library mounted an exhibition honoring Cy Young, the right-handed pitcher who won a record 511 major league games from 1890 through 1911, playing for the Cleveland Spiders, St. Louis Nationals, Boston Red Sox, Cleveland Indians, and Boston Braves.

The exhibit, which was scheduled to travel around the state, included some of the baseball uniforms Cy had worn on the diamond. To kick it off, a local television station offered a round trip for two anywhere in the U.S.A., courtesy of Continental Airlines, to the seventh caller able to come up with Cy's full name -- Denton True Young.

Not to be outdone, somebody in baseball-mad Cleveland planted actual advance tickets to long sold-out Indians games in the collections of the magnificent new addition to the ornate old public library -- a towering structure of recent construction named in honor of Louis B. Stokes, a popular and long-serving African-American congressman.

"Whoever did that is a genius in Cleveland psychology!" said Hawley Short, reading to his wife an account of how the library was inundated during the lunch hour by hundreds of fans bereft of tickets in a city whose new ballpark had been sold out since the day it opened. In a futile effort to stem the tide, the librarian, an avid devotee of the sport and not above doing a little hunting herself on her own free time, had posted a copy of the letter from the anonymous donor at the entrance.

This advised that his generosity had extended to just twenty tickets. "There are None to games with the despised New York Yankees," the letter said. "I just could not bring myself to part with these, but there are several to games with the Boston Red Sox." This was sufficient to stimulate record

17

patronage at the library even long after all twenty tickets were found.

As the daffodils came and went and the star magnolia in his front yard put out its blossoms before clothing itself for the summer in shiny green leaves, Hawley was pleased to read that his fellow Ohioans had acted with special generosity to promote the reading of books by some of the state's leading literary lights. These included Sherwood Anderson from Camden, chronicler of the damage done to the social structure of Ohio's small towns by the forces of industrialization; Ambrose Bierce, born on a poor farm in hard-scrabble Meigs County -- the crusty satirist and author of one of Hawley's favorite books, The Devil's Dictionary -- Louis Bromfield of Mansfield, the novelist and progressive farmer; and Toni Morrison, a contemporary African-American novelist from Lorain, who won the Nobel Prize for Literature in 1993.

Someone in Toledo, who had checked out a book by David Ross Locke, one of Abraham Lincoln's favorite humorists, was rewarded with a ten-dollar bill.

"That's certainly worth a chuckle," said Hawley to his wife. "I wonder if anyone besides whoever won the ten dollars and yours truly remembers that Locke wrote under the pseudonym Petroleum V. Nasby."

"But, look-ee here!" he exclaimed, "someone down in Columbus has inserted twenty dollar bills in books by another of our state's humorists, James Thurber.

"Must have cost a pretty penny!" he exclaimed, "as there are something like 453 Thurber entries in the computerized card catalogue Neal Barker showed me the other day over at the college, when he was teaching me how to run my new word processor.

"Now, many of those are various editions of a single work. But even so, if you take into account all the books in which Thurber's short stories or drawings appear, you are still left with at least a couple of hundred, which means by my calculation that someone has invested at least four thousand dollars in promoting the reading of Thurber. Wonder who that might be?"

"Remember what fun we had visiting the old Thurber homestead in Columbus last summer," Mrs. Short interjected, "the way the gabled attic had been restored as a suite for a visiting Writer in Residence. I can't think of a more appropriate way to honor a literary man's memory...."

18

"You're right about that, but I got to get going," said Hawley, swinging his well-worn, waterproof green book bag over his shoulder. "I'm off for a special meeting of the council, to discuss all the implications of what's going on."

Lydia McGovern, who arrived shortly before him, had scarcely entered the library when her ears picked up a high, shrill sound emitted from the table where a young boy, Braxton Augustus, was cranking the handle on the microfilm reader.

She touched him gently on the shoulder, smiled and said, "the machine you are using is making a wee bit of a noise." The youngster was so intent on his research that he recoiled on his chair, startled, and immediately made effort at apology.

Lydia waved it aside. "Not your fault! Heavens no! But if you don't mind I have a can of oil on the back of my bicycle. Mind if I retrieve it?"

"No, maam, not at all," said Braxton.

Once she had put a few drops on the crank, she departed with a smile, and Braxton rolled the film on noiselessly.

Meantime, María Álvarez had arrived, and headed for the Ladies Room, down the corridor off the far side of the main reading room. Going and coming her nose was offended by a hideous smell whose source was obvious -- a foul-bodied street person who had commandeered a large table near the corridor, his worldly possessions in a large green plastic bag.

María squirmed at the disgusting spectacle, a grown young man of about her own age in rags and tatters -- idly, as it seemed to her at a glance, turning the pages of a thick tabloid newspaper. He smirked whenever something engaged his passing attention, and continuously scratched himself on his behind and worked jaws that housed a mouthful of dirty teeth.

Muttering "Madre de Dios!" under her breath, María could not resist giving him a piece of her mind.

"Why must you bring your smell into this place?" she asked, pushing up her glasses on her nose, her large eyes flashing with anger, "this library which so many people have worked so long and hard to make attractive?"

The words tumbled out involuntarily. When she realized how loudly she was speaking, María was fearful lest she disturb the peace of other

19

readers, who had arranged themselves, she noticed, so as to be as far away as possible from the object of her contempt. But as she spoke, she could sense that they applauded her action.

Emboldened by this tacit show of support, María continued in a loud voice: "See how everybody else is offended by your presence?" This outburst elicited a sound of muffled laughter from the onlookers. But the street person merely ignored María, and indeed her very existence in that time and place, in favor of staring single-mindedly -- if indeed he had a mind -- at the pages of the newspaper.

María marched off, resolutely planting her delicate small feet as noisily as possible on the floor, and joined the members of the Council in the corridor leading to the conference room.

"Poor man!" said Charles Whitney, who had witnessed the encounter from afar.

"First street person we've had," said Louella Winters, "strange that he should show up just now, when there is so much excitement in the air; though you know a library, as someone said, is just an extension of the sidewalk, the last place in America, where a homeless person can go, and be welcomed, no questions asked, as long as he doesn't disturb anybody.

"He's not from around here. I wonder what he's up to? Nobody knows who he is, and as you saw he's not very friendly, is he?"

"On a more positive note," said Neal Barker, changing the subject abruptly: "The boy using the microfilm reader -- you'll never guess what he's researching."

"Well, c'mon, out with it," said the ever-inquisitive Lydia McGovern.

"He's looking up a newspaper story involving his father, about a bungled bank robbery here in Plymouth that landed his old man in jail where, as I understand it, he is working in the library."

"Didn't know they had libraries in prisons," said Hawley Short. "That's encouraging."

"I've got something else that may tickle you, Hawley," said Neal Barker, who led off the discussion of the many and marvelous ways people around Ohio were helping to promote reading by showing the members of the council a lottery ticket he had just purchased.

"Now, what you have to do is scratch the boxes on this little card for which I paid one dollar. If you match the first and last names of a well-known Ohio author, then you win the prize indicated in this other little box."

As everybody leaned forward around the table Neal scratched the surface of the card with a dime, slowly uncovering the first word, which was Zane.

"That would be Zane as in Zane Grey of Zanesville, Ohio," blurted out Hawley Short, "the most popular author of Westerns our country has ever produced. Why you know he wrote more than 50 novels, which sold in the aggregate more than 40 million copies. I wish some of our authors today would emulate his example, and provide readers with stories emphasizing the intelligent use of our country's resources and high moral values like he did in Riders of the Purple Sage which, if memory serves, was published back in 1912."

"Thanks for the nuggets from your inexhaustible store of trivia," said Neal.

"Now look! If I uncover his last name, Grey, in one of the five remaining boxes, why then I'll win a prize. Let's see: Paul, Ambrose, Anderson, James, and Dunbar. Bingo! Paul Dunbar, a fellow African-American. Let's see what I have won. Aw nuts, it's just another ticket."

"But a significant victory it is," said Hawley Short, "as Paul Laurence -- it's a pity the ticket lacked space for his middle name -- Dunbar, the Dayton, Ohio poet, who published twelve books from 1896-1905, before his life was cut short at age 34. That's more than any African-American author had published up until 1950, as I read somewhere the other day."

"Well, this little ticket is not very sophisticated," said Neal, ignoring Hawley's pedantic thrust, "but it has given me some thoughts on a possible way to go in mapping out a computer literacy game. It's also an indication that the politicians down in Columbus are aware of what we're doing, that when the time comes they may be favorably disposed if someone can come up with a viable idea."

When the meeting broke up Neal saw that Braxton Augustus was still at work on the microfilm reader.

"I think I'll just see if he could use some help, maybe even a little mentoring," he said to María at the door of the library.

"I'm sure you can help him a lot, Neal. But watch out for that street person in the corner."

María had no idea why the spectacle of that man had so disturbed her, but it had. For the rest of the day she couldn't get him out of her mind, try as she might. He even intruded himself into her restless sleep.

This may have accounted for why she arose even earlier than usual the following morning for her job at the small Convenience store where she had been working for three years after graduating from the local community college, to support her further education. Somehow the street person had stirred feelings in her that she would have been hard put to explain to anyone, even the priest to whom she regularly confessed her sins.

On awakening, she dawdled longer than usual in the shower of her cozy, small apartment, gave her hair a few extra strokes after thoroughly drying it off, and exercised special care in the selection of her attire, even rummaging around in the darkness of her closet for a pair of shoes whose color would compliment that of her dress. Before going out the door, she put a pair of silver bracelets on her wrists, which jangled as she walked.

In her devotion to the work ethic María was an apt representative of the millions of Mexican-born people who have swarmed across the border and by their presence reinvigorated the ambience of places as far-removed as Plymouth and Los Angeles. Without their fresh energy many Americans would have long ago found it difficult to have a house painted at a reasonable cost, or an automobile repaired, or the weeds removed from their gardens.

For María, like other children of these newcomers to America, the experience of growing up as a member of a downtrodden immigrant minority was fast receding into her subconscious. Still, today, for reasons she could not fathom, she remembered the promise she had made as a small girl to her grandfather before leaving Mexico, that if she ever married, there would be live music by Mariachis.

For some reason she thought of that vow, as she prepared for the morning rush at the Convenience store. Through the large plate glass window, she caught a fleeting glimpse of Lydia McGovern riding her bicycle down Hayes Street, and waved to her. But she was sure that Lydia didn't see her gesture, so intent was her hooded figure on reaching the small Episcopal Church located directly across the busy thoroughfare

22

which was already groaning under the weight of large trucks, huge eight and ten-wheel semis.

Meantime, María had a cheerful greeting for the building contractors and construction men. Many of them were Hispanic immigrants like herself, anxious to wolf down a pastry and some steaming coffee before setting off for a long day's labor. She felt a deep and special sense of compassion for members of the latest immigrant wave from Central America, driven upon America's shores by political upheaval and fratricidal strife back home.

As they lined up for coffee, they seemed to her pitifully vulnerable, disoriented, sleepwalkers, rudely wakened as from a dream, to find themselves strangers in a cold and cheerless climate. Strangers, moreover, in a culture where the dental "thank you" had replaced the soft sibilant "graçias" of the lands of their birth, where the sweet coffee from their homelands had been transformed by inept roasting into something that tasted awful.

Amid such depressing thoughts and still unsettled by her run-in with the street person, María was happy to see Hawley Short's cheerful countenance and listen to his recital of familiar words:

"As per the standing order, you are not permitted to sell me a doughnut, even if I plead with you to do so," he said, as he paid for one of the three copies of The New York Times that the store stocked.

As usual, he had arrived on foot from his home a couple of blocks distant, having been up already for a couple of hours, pounding away on yet another novel on the new word processor Neal Barker had helped him install.

"Oh, yes, I've written a number of them," he had told María previously, when he was using a typewriter. "Fortunately, I've had the good sense to throw them away before showing them to anybody, but this one" (something he had said of several of the ones he had discarded) "this one may prove a winner, if only because the word processor corrects my bad spelling and underlines in red my more egregious grammatical mistakes for correction."

"I'm sure it will be," said María, as Hawley grinned from ear to ear. "Positive!"

Chapter 4

PUBLIC DEMANDS

As Hawley Short headed home, a low-flying jet roared overhead with an aspiring writer like himself aboard though he was much younger and recovering from a dreadful hangover.

"That makes two of us," Brian Hedley muttered to himself, when the pilot announced an unscheduled stop in Cleveland "due to a mechanical problem."

Once the plane had rolled to a stop, Brian dashed into the terminal seeking relief, something to ease the pounding in his head. His misery, as he well knew, was self-inflicted, the result of a weekend of wretched over-indulgence in New York where he had exhausted himself under the sheets, making love between tumblers full of bourbon with a not-very-attractive woman.

But maybe it would prove worth it, for the lady in question had arranged for him to pitch an idea for a television series with her boss in Los Angeles, Mr. Vance LePage, the number three or four person -- Brian couldn't remember which -- with a television production studio.

Brian had not a clue as to what that idea might be, but he would think of something. He always had in the past, though nothing had yet worked out. No matter! This time it would be different. Like droves of young people before him, who had flocked to Hollywood, seeking fame and money -- enough for a piano-shaped swimming pool -- he had the gambler's sense of confidence before each spin of the roulette wheel, when every number is a good number up until the second the wheel stops.

While downing an Alka-Seltzer, Brian, a native of Independence, Ohio, picked up a newspaper someone had discarded on the counter. He would have just seven hours to come up with an idea, and only five minutes to pitch it with Vance LePage the lady under the sheets had admonished him,

24

when he had come up for air and bourbon.

Meantime, Brian, a thoughtful young man in his early thirties, puzzled over the bizarre nature of his chosen profession. For openers, he wondered why it was that he had to go to New York to make an appointment with someone in L.A.? Why would anyone in his right mind invest money in a television production company when most of them went broke before they produced a single flickering image on anybody's screen? And -- as he idly eyed the newspaper on the counter -- why would anybody put dollar bills into library books?

"Hey, that's it!" he exclaimed excitedly. "What I'm looking for! A pitchable idea! Something just nutty enough to be a winner."

As his flight became airborne and passed over the level lands of northeast Ohio and the library down below, which could be the means of his deliverance from abject screen-writer poverty, Brian waved off the stewardess, pulled out his tray, and commenced scribbling in a blind fury on the margins of the discarded newspaper: "Friends of the Library, the pilot for a television series based on what actually happened at the Public Library of Plymouth, Ohio, in the spring of 1998."

Then Brian plunged ahead with the task of working out a cast for the show that would reflect in microcosm the ethnic composition of the prime-time television-viewing audience. Everything else was secondary to that, putting up on the screen characters viewers could easily identify with people like themselves.

As Brian bent to this labor, Louella Winters was waging her daily uphill struggle to satisfy public demands. For people in town were looking to the library to satisfy a bewildering and ever-multiplying assortment of tasks (many of them previously carried out by other agencies). As a result, Louella, like librarians elsewhere, devoted much of her time to listening to appeals from various groups and individuals desirous of involving the Plymouth library in their causes and activities.

Her first visitors on that morning in June - the day that creative inspiration struck Brian Hedley on high -- were from the Plymouth Gay and Lesbian Alliance, who had set up an appointment to discuss the fight against AIDS and the special needs of their group's members. Louella received them hospitably. Without revealing her own sexual orientation   (it was none of their business, she thought) -- Louella pointed out that the library was always happy to lend its backing to campaigns that would lead to improved community health.

The library, she noted, regularly made its facilities available for tuberculosis and blood pressure screening. A mobile team from the hospital in town used library space monthly to collect blood donated by patrons. The local cancer society held periodical clinics at the library, advertising to the community the symptoms of the disease, and an annual weeklong anti-smoking campaign that targeted teenagers. This was not to mention the library's involvement all year around in federal, state, and local efforts as part of the nation's war on drugs.

As Louella spoke, her visitors seemed impatient, their eyes and ears open wide to detect in her voice, manner, or body language the least possible -- indeed the most minute -- expression of the slightest antipathy on her part toward their lifestyle. Once reassured by her obvious, cheerful competence, they launched into their agenda, demanding first of all that the Plymouth library, "like themselves," as one of them joked, "come out of the closet," purchase more books and videos on gay subjects, and participate fully in Gay Pride Week.

Moreover, they urged that the library set up permanently a table where people could obtain literature highlighting their lifestyle, chronicling the ongoing national struggle by gay and lesbian couples to obtain conjugal rights, and, most important of all, materials describing how to prevent AIDS. For this purpose they urge that the library pass out free condoms to patrons at the circulation desk, no questions asked.

They hastened to assure her that their organization would keep the library well supplied with these disease-preventing devices. Finally, they asked that the library provide a meeting room equipped with a VCR, a slide projector and, if possible, a moving-picture projector accommodating both 16 and 35 millimeter films (plus a staff member to operate it), for the regular, monthly get-togethers of the Plymouth Gay and Lesbian Alliance.

Louella was not surprised by their requests. They were, it seemed to her, entirely reasonable as seen from their particular perspective. Nor were they much different from those people are making of libraries on an enormous range of matters, from joining the fight to save endangered species, promoting energy conservation awareness, or holding seminars on investing in the stock market to coping with stress, infestations of ladybugs or household mold.

Foremost among those making demands, she told her visitors, were the single moms and dads in a nation where about half of all marriages don't last, and for whom the library represents a sort of tax-supported parental partner or baby-sitter. Responding to their pressure, she said, the Plymouth library had extended its range of children's activities to stratospheric proportions. There was instruction in origami and finger-painting, dental hygiene classes where free toothbrushes and toothpaste were passed out courtesy of pharmaceutical companies, and on and on the list. There were even special sessions conducted by local police and firemen, who instructed children on how to thwart a kidnapper or safely exit a burning home. Moreover, the library had mounted a special bulletin board, which was updated daily, with photos of missing children from Nome to Tallahassee.

Nor was Louella at all taken aback, she said to her gay and lesbian visitors, by their desire to involve the library in accomplishing their goal.

"Why even the Internal Revenue Service does that," she joked, before describing how the library set aside two special tables from January through April of each year, stocked with federal, state and municipal tax forms in English and Spanish. "You may be interested to learn that about 15% of the population here in Plymouth is comprised of Hispanics, and a good many of them don't read English," she said.

She also noted how the library stocked a full set of the explanatory booklets the IRS issues by way of providing taxpayer guidance on how to fill out the various forms. "At the peak of the tax preparation season," she added, "we also have several volunteers on hand -- including two or three fluent in Spanish -- to help patrons of the library fill out their forms, though I must say we have had occasional complaints from people who make their living doing this. This is not to mention how two people in our reference department have received special training that enables them to help people who want to file their taxes electronically -- something that will be absorbing more of their time in the years ahead.

"We do what we must in the case of federal agencies, as, for example, on election days, when about a quarter of the people in town come to the library to vote," she said, "and we do what we can for all non-governmental organizations and groups. But I have to tell you that we receive so many requests to involve us and make use of our facilities in non-library activities that we ask that each such request be submitted in writing. This should include supporting documentation showing why the library, of all the possible venues here in Plymouth, including schools, churches, and the community center, should undertake to provide the particular support requested."

"Oh, come off it!" interjected one of her butch visitors, "you know how important AIDS is."

"That has nothing to do with what I am telling you," Louella replied resolutely, her face carefully reflecting the natural offense she felt at the tone of the remark. "This is a policy which was adopted long ago by our Friends Council. It is not directed against you or any organization seeking to do good in the community. It is just that there are limits to our capacity to help, as I'm sure you must understand."

Her remark seemed reasonable to at least three of her visitors, who prevailed upon the fourth to shut up, and the meeting ended amicably. The leader of the group thanked her "for seeing them on what was doubtless a busy day," and said that she would be hearing from them in writing in due course.

Rising to shake their hands, Louella accompanied them to the door of her office, where a blind young couple was waiting to see her, their Labrador guide-dogs snoozing under the table where the new fax machine would soon be located. Louella, it is worth noting, was terribly afraid of big dogs, having been bitten on the hand as a young girl by a German Shepherd, when she was camping with her family in Wisconsin.

It was only after the docile Labradors had rearranged themselves under the window in her office that she felt entirely comfortable, and turned her full attention to her attractive callers who had come well prepared.

They had arranged the meeting, they said, to discuss ways the library might better serve the needs of handicapped people like themselves. The young man began by reading from a list of requests, filed on his laptop, which handled Braille. "First of all," he said, "we would like to call your attention to the need for a special, sound-proof room where blind people can listen to works recorded for their use by volunteers on special machines, equipped to handle cassettes and disks. This will require at least one, and preferably several, new players, he noted, as recordings for the blind are made at non-commercial speeds to prevent their recreational use by sighted people."

While he paused to bring up some other notes on his laptop, Louella noted that, of course, they must be familiar with the Library of Congress program to provide recordings for the blind, how she had visited one of the 50 regional centers the Library has situated around the country, especially for such physically handicapped people. The Plymouth library, she added, regularly borrowed recordings from these centers for the use of local patrons, as indeed works in Braille, as requested by people like themselves.

They nodded and the young lady, who was endowed with a radiant smile, suggested that in view of the special needs of people like herself, the Plymouth library might want to assign some special member of the staff to attend to their needs, or indeed add a blind person to the staff.

"I'll be happy to look into that," Louella said, wondering if the young woman might have herself in mind for such a job. "It's certainly a worthwhile activity. But I must caution you that we are stretched pretty thin right now you might say even beyond the limit of what we can reasonably provide in the way of service to our patrons in an orderly and efficient manner."

Subtly to emphasize the point, Louella asked whether they might like some coffee, saying: "I have had to make it myself, since I lost my secretary, owing to a budget cut," before excusing herself briefly to retrieve a tray with cups and milk and sugar. When she returned, the earnest young man called her attention to a recent news story about a library for blind people in New York City. "This library," he read aloud, "has the most fully automated system in use by any library for the blind. Moreover, sightless patrons can even browse the stacks, finding their way about by Braille signs and markings on the spines of books.

"And listen to this!" he said, quoting again from the newspaper article. "There are lounge chairs, tables and study carrels wired for audio playback equipment and closed-circuit television magnifiers that enlarge the print for those whose sight is only impaired, and for children suffering vision problems there is a room with large, stuffed lions, bears and pandas, and a piano."

"I don't know if all our other patrons would appreciate a piano," interjected Louella, and they all had a pleasant laugh.

But the young man persisted in reading more from the story. "Revolving storage carousels -- like clothing racks in dry cleaning establishments hold returned books, most of which have already been requested by other patrons. The computer compares requests with returns and then generates mailing labels for the items to be shipped."

"And why not the dry cleaning as well?" Louella observed playfully, and they all had another hearty laugh as the meeting wound down, and Louella rose to see them and their dogs out the front door via the special handicapped ramp, which the library had recently installed.

While bidding them goodbye at the bottom of the ramp, she was accosted by a man with a heavy display case, who asked in a rude tone of voice: "Say, you're the librarian here, aren't you?"

"There is no other word for it," Louella replied, "and I'll bet there is something I can do for you."

"As a matter of fact there is," he said, introducing himself as a travelling salesman. "You see, I want the library to buy more 'books to drive by.' You know, the kind you play on a cassette deck while you are driving to soak up a little culture. I'm on the road all the time, a couple hundred thousand miles a year. To kill the time I like to listen to books on tapes. But I've already gone through those here in your library. So I'm here to ask you, how about buying some more? "By the way, I really enjoyed William Manchester reading his <u>The Glory and the Dream</u> -- nearly 60 hours of it. It got me all the way from here to Dallas. What a story!"

"I'll make a note of your suggestion when I get back to my office," said Louella. "I'll put it on the same list with a request from some of our seniors for more large-print books and another from children for more pop-up books."

"Pop-up books?" said the salesman. "What in the H E double toothpicks are they?"

"Well, they don't have many words," Louella explained, "but the children love them. You see, when you open the book a scene pops up. With every new page there is a new scene in three dimensions. On another day I'll be happy to show your some of them," she said, politely excusing herself.

"Well, I'll be darned," said the salesman. 'I'll definitely be back to have a look."

When Hawley Short reached the library a few moments later, he could see that Louella had made it only as far as the corridor leading to her office before being besieged by six very large, leather-jacketed youths, their hair so long that it was difficult to pick out the girls from the boys.

In loud and peremptory tones, they were renewing their demand that the library acquire X-rated videos. The leader of the deputation, which had arrived aboard a fleet of Harley-Davidsons that were blocking the handicapped ramp, was citing the Constitution's first amendment guarantee of free speech and the fact that he and his friends were all taxpayers, as Hawley arrived on the scene.

Moreover, the black-jacketed youth continued, after quickly surveying his shaggy compadres, "we all voted in favor of the recent library bond issue," though Hawley doubted it.

Seeing Louella thus embattled and getting the gist of their complaint, Hawley rushed fearlessly into the fray. "Look here," he said, "my name is Hawley Short. I'm a member in good standing of the Friends of this library, and I'm glad I arrived in time to give you a piece of my mind. But before I do that, would you please remove your motorcycles from the ramp constructed at considerable expense for the handicapped, and park them in the lot set aside for that purpose."

Hesitantly and dragging their boots across the floor, the youths shuffled out the front door to comply with his order, affording Louella a chance to express her gratitude. "Sure glad to see you, Hawley. They were really being, if I may say so, rudely insistent that we acquire X-rated videos."

"Think nothing of it," Hawley replied affably. "And forgive me for barging in like that, but it certainly looked from the distance of the main portal as if you were facing an unequal foe. Now, if you will permit me I'd like to borrow your conference room, and some of your coffee and cups. I've got a little plan. We'll kill them with kindness."

Louella nodded appreciatively, and once the leatherjackets had gathered about the table, she popped in with a freshly brewed pot of coffee: "Now, if you'll excuse me, I have a mountain of things to attend to. I'll leave you in Mr. Short's good hands."

For nearly an hour Hawley expounded upon the history of libraries in Ohio. "By chance," he began, "I have just finished reading a beautifully-bound book called Sketches of Ohio Libraries published back in 1902.

Many of our state's early libraries owed their establishment to women who organized little collections of books, which they loaned out, within their homes. In support of this activity their men-folk contributed the pelts of animals, which were traded back east for books. That's why they called one of our state's first public libraries, which was established in Ames township in 1804, 'The Coonskin Library.' "

Whether his visitors got the point he doubted, but Hawley plunged ahead with his rambling narrative: "You will be interested to learn that this library where we speak is one of II5 such libraries built later on in Ohio thanks to the generosity of Andrew Carnegie. Perhaps you are not familiar with that name," he said.

"Well, you should be. Between I898 and I918 this gentleman, a Scotch immigrant, who had become very wealthy in the steel business down in Pittsburgh, helped finance a total of 2,509 libraries worldwide, 1,679 of them in the U.S.A. Almost all of those he helped build here in Ohio are still standing. Three-quarters of them are still in use as libraries, like this one here in Plymouth; most of the others have become offices for municipalities, colleges, doctors or lawyers."

Having thus added to their store of knowledge, Hawley went on to point out to his soon-glazed-over audience all the various constituencies the Plymouth library served, how the library's budget always lagged behind the public demands placed upon it, how all of the library's various constituencies, including some new ones every day, were insisting that the library buy this or that.

He discussed recent advances in technology which had further burdened the library's slim pocketbook, how music lovers, for example, were now insisting that the library not just maintain and enlarge its lending collections of records, but buy all the latest compact disks, as well. Movie-lovers like themselves, he pointed out, were insisting that the library collect all of the classics, as well as the latest popular releases, and would soon be insisting that the library acquire digitalized versions of films to play upon the expensive new DVD machines which were coming onto the market.

"Now, of course," he emphasized, "the library is no friend of censorship, nor does it wish to infringe on anyone's right to view whatever he or she wants to within the sanctity of his or her own residence. But there was always the possibility that some impressionable youngster might check out an X-rated movie, and the library would soon be hearing from the parents. Or, are you proposing that this library, like a bar serving liquor or a grocery store selling cigarettes, check the I.D.'s of all those partaking of its provender?" The more he warmed to the subject, the more eloquent Hawley became, quoting snippets from ancient and modern verse, which he had committed to memory while shaving in the morning from paper Post-its he stuck on the mirror the night before. It was only once he was fully persuaded that he had sufficiently wearied what gray matter had survived the Age of Sex and Violence in which these youths had grown up, in the strained effort to fathom what he was talking about, that Hawley issued a challenge.

"I'll gladly buy a tank full of high-octane gas for anyone among you who will read A Confederacy of Dunces by John Kennedy Toole, and tell me that in his or her considered opinion it is not as good as any X-rated video you may have seen. Here again is the title of the book," Hawley continued, writing it down, "and here's my phone number."

As he wrote he described how the novel had only seen the light of day owing to the persistence of the author's mother, the author himself having committed suicide, presumably because of his inability to find a publisher for his manuscript.

The girl, who earlier had giggled over a piece of verse he had quoted, was mildly intrigued and accepted the piece of paper from his hands.

Whereupon Hawley launched into part two of his little plan, to wit, to inform them that the library could use their help in rounding up books for the book sale that would be held three or four months hence in the fall.

The heavily bearded leader of the group, after having cast an eye around the table at his companions, their heads spinning from Hawley's recital, raised his hand for silence, and said: "You tell us when. We'll collect 'em."

"Splendid!" Hawley said, and the meeting shortly broke up in friendly fashion. But not before he had pumped the hand of each of those on hand, and said: "I want to thank you for hearing me out. I hope that you will help put out the word among your compadres. I'll put you in touch with the volunteers who will be overseeing the book sale -- whoever they may be. I know they will appreciate your assistance in gathering books offered by a good many older people, who contact us by phone -- shut-ins, for the most part, too feeble to deliver the books in person."

At the door the girl who had giggled said: "Say I heard on television that people discovered money in some of the books in this library. Is that so?"

"Indeed, it is!" Hawley replied, smiling broadly.

"Cool!" exclaimed the biker chick. "Maybe there's a little something in this one," she said, holding up the paper on which he had written the title.

"That book is out just now," said Hawley, telling a little fib, "but I'm sure if you stop by next week you can have a look-see."

Chapter 5

Book Plates

" You almost ran me down!" said Hawley Short, stepping aside as Lydia McGovern braked her bicycle to a stop at the curb in front of the coffee shop on Main Street. "You really must be more careful in the way you career around town on that conveyance. The Missus and I often say a prayer for you. Bicycles, as she was saying just the other day, have no seat belts, though perhaps corporate America can figure out a way to provide them, assuming the price is right, and Congress passes a law requiring them.

"Now, if you will afford me the pleasure of your company, I'll gladly fetch and pay for a pot of tea for you and a mug of coffee for me," he said with a funny little bow in her direction.

"Perfect," said Lydia. "I want to show you something."

As she arranged her possessions at a sidewalk table, Hawley went inside and procured some herbal tea for her, strong African coffee for himself, and a plate of scones to share, with plenty of blackberry jam and cream cheese -- at a price he considered exorbitant.

Like Hawley, Lydia could be counted upon for a rambling lead into whatever she had on her mind. This morning was no exception. She began by describing how she had discovered the truth of what he had demonstrated in putting dollar bills in books: that people of Plymouth would turn out in droves whenever there was a chance of getting something for nothing.

She recalled a cold and rainy morning, before the weather had taken a turn for the better. How the line of cars had stretched for more than a mile near her apartment, when the municipal government offered the local citizenry free buckets for recycling some of their trash -- bottles and the like.

"People in Plymouth," she emphasized, describing the hideous crush of cars on streets covered with ice, "will turn out for anything that is free!"

"No argument there," said Hawley. "Those buckets are mighty useful, too. The Missus and I use them for collecting pine cones and sea shells up on the shore of Lake Erie, and I confess to having persuaded our local authorities to give us three instead of the allotted two."

"Then you are a case in point," said Lydia, smiling and spreading out on the table an advertisement she had sketched out for the Plymouth Gazette.

It said "FREE" in large block letters at both the top and bottom of the page. In between and in smaller letters, it read: "You are cordially invited to place a Bookplate in memory of a friend or relative or loved one in one of the books newly acquired by the Plymouth Public Library. Those interested should stop in at the Library and make known the particulars of those they wish to honor."

"Great idea!" Hawley enthused. "Why with that addition to our program we Friends of the Plymouth Library will be affording patrons services extending from the cradle to the grave, so to speak. In confirmation of what a wise man once told me: to wit, that if you exclude libraries, the rest of everything here on planet earth is, in a manner of speaking, just so much overhead.

"By the way, I'm more than willing to share the cost of placing this notice."

"Much appreciated," said Lydia, "but that won't be necessary. When I stopped by the bank and showed it to Charles Whitney, he insisted on paying for it himself on one condition -- that the Gazette devote an entire page to it."

"You make me out a piker!" Hawley chortled good-naturedly, "though Charles's generosity does not surprise me. Of all the members of our Council I think it is he who has the deepest affection for books. His wife told me that he thinks they saved his life, when he was suffering from bouts of deep depression during his lengthy ordeal at the veterans hospital.

"But on a brighter note -- if your marvelous idea works out, as I think it will, in time perhaps we can get Preston Myers to expand upon it -- he's always bugging Louella about making the library more 'market-oriented.' No, don't laugh, that's the exact phrase he uses, as do a great many people smarter than our dim-witted Preston.

"You may be amused to learn that he recently sent Louella this newspaper clipping, of which she made me a copy, knowing I'd get some fun out of it. It's headlined 'Ohio Libraries Are Shelving Their Stuffy Image For Broader Appeal.'

"Look here," Hawley continued, "there is an accompanying photo showing a magician with a funny nose, who had children cheering at one of our libraries, according to the caption. In the text of the article Preston highlighted in yellow the following passage: 'Not long ago, a raucous magic show would have been unthinkable inside a public library. But these are different times. Faced with increased competition and the changing needs of patrons, more and more libraries are modeling themselves as entertainment venues and cultural bazaars. Patrons can freely sample programming that ranges from belly dancing to plant propagation.'"

"You don't mean it, Preston can't be serious," said Lydia.

"Oh, yes he is!" snapped Hawley. "Nor is he the only one who thinks that way.

"So what I'm suggesting is that we somehow plant in Preston's head that when people drop by to inquire about bookplates, we can hit 'em up for a membership in the Friends. It only costs five bucks for a family, three for a single, and two for a senior, which reminds me I don't think we have changed our membership dues since the Great Depression.

"We could also 'program' Preston, if you get what I mean, to suggest that we encourage people to insert bookplates to mark birthdays, Mother's Day, wedding anniversaries -- allow their creativity full rein in designing plates in accord with their own proclivities, which in Preston's case might mean bookplates with belly dancers.

"What I'm saying, Lydia, is that you have hit upon something that has what would seem to this gray old head a double-edge. It would help get the Prestons of the world off Louella's back and, at the same time, bring people into the library for the right reasons, and I congratulate you on it!"

Lydia blushed, consulted her watch, and hastily excused herself: "Thanks for the tea and scones."

Fortified by his good opinion and that of other members of the Friends Council, Preston Myers, as Hawley had predicted, was positively ecstatic about it and rose to the bait of figuring out additional ways to embellish upon her idea -- Lydia delivered the advertisement to the Gazette There an elderly copy editor, wearing a green eye-shade, the trademark of his profession, scanned her text approvingly.

"With all the late relatives I've got," he said, "I'll be the first in line. Trouble is that most of them never read a book in their lives."

"Well, they've got plenty of time now," Lydia observed.

Once the ad had appeared, Lydia basked in the congratulations of her many friends all around Plymouth, who knew of her hand in it, even Neal Barker, who had only one small suggestion: "You seem to have forgotten that people may want to put some sort of bookplate into something other than a book, a CD or a videotape or a DVD, for example."

"To quote Hawley Short, 'I can't do it all myself,'" Lydia said.

"You're right about that. If you'll permit me I'll get right to work on that," Neal said affably. He added: "You know Lydia, we can use the information people give us, when they sign up for a bookplate, to start a data bank in the Genealogy and Local History department, and thereby revolutionize our collection of local vital statistics."

"That's certainly an interesting twist, Neal," Lydia said, secure in the knowledge that this idea would meet with firm rejection from Mary Mountfort, the head of that department, who had alone, of all the people on the library staff, thus far successfully resisted all attempts to "compu-terrorize," as she put it, her domain.

"With friends like you, who needs enemies?" said Louella Winters in greeting Lydia at the entrance of the library on the day the bookplate offer went into effect. In disbelief they gazed at the long line of people which stretched for hundreds of yards across the nearby grassy park.

Some clutched lists of deceased relatives gleaned from family Bibles and faded obituaries. Others brought multiple copies of bookplates they had themselves designed, complete with grainy photos of the late lamented. The bookplates were awash in trite sentiments. Some were accompanied by graphics, like one for a late professor at the local college, which included a reproduction of the frontispiece from one of his favorite books. Another local scholar was memorialized with an etching of a medieval library, showing a monk dressed in a heavy fur coat against the cold, reading by candlelight.

One bookplate had a sketch of a castle on a hill and the legend "Not a failure but a low aim is a crime." Another had a brief biography of a young man killed in the Second World War, followed by an exhortation to the readers of the book in which it was affixed, "to think about some of the great problems about which he thought, and strive in whatever ways may for them be possible or necessary, for the maintenance and the perfecting of American democracy, and for the achievement of a peaceful world."

The Plymouth Gay and Lesbian Alliance had rushed into print bookplates in pink with the movement's white triangle for the special use of its members. Several of them were standing in the long, long line.

"I must confess that I have never felt such a sense of fulfillment," said Lydia to Louella, as they surveyed the scene. "In a funny way, the bookplates are a sort of sweet revenge against the Episcopal hierarchy for its so-called 'updating' of the Book of Common Prayer. You know how much that upset me, the dumb-ing down of the stately language of the book that was given to me when I was confirmed."

"Here I, a simple librarian, was looking forward to a quiet day," said Louella, "and you have put upon us the task of becoming Plymouth's memory lane, as well as place of observance for those disaffected, like yourself, by today's manifestations of so-called organized religion.

"And why not," said Louella, giving Lydia a hug. "What else, other than some divine spirit, could have inspired some of the books commonly found in the shelves of any public library, this one included? For people, I hasten to add, like yourself, for whom reading is not just an idle pursuit, like golf or bridge, but a vocation."

"Thank you for that comforting thought," said Lydia, smiling, as Louella drifted off to work, mercifully in ignorance of the further disruptions in her busy schedule that lay ahead, as a result of a five-minute meeting between Brian Hedley and Vance LePage out in California -- at the latter's home in Malibu.

Upon arrival in Los Angeles, Brian had hurriedly transcribed the notes he had made while airborne onto a single, double-spaced page. He had then hastily shaved, brushed his teeth, and put on some Hollywood-style casual clothes for his impending meeting with Mr. Big.

"Now what was I supposed to say?" he asked himself as he drove up in his beat-up old Chevy Impala to the fortified tower that guarded the compound where LePage lived.

Pulling to a stop, he got out and was frisked by a beefy guard, while a bomb-sniffing German Shepherd checked out his car.

"I wouldn't advise you to pat him!" the guard warned from behind silvered sunglasses, as the German Shepherd pawed about the back seat.

"Now who do you want to see?"

"I have an appointment with Mr. Vance LePage," Brian said. "Stella arranged it from New York."

The guard, looking as if he wanted to signal the dog to attack, fingered the flap over his revolver, and said: "Well, I guess it's okay if she says so. It's the third house on the right. You can park this bucket of bolts in front of Mr. LePage's place for six minutes, that allows you a half minute to get in and another half-minute to get out. After that I can't guarantee either your life or this hunk of junk."

At the front door Brian punched in the security code, which he had committed to memory. Hearing a buzzer, he entered the palatial residence to find LePage, who had just emerged from his swimming pool, toweling off his thick torso.

Brian declined his offer of coffee (he thought it would be too time-consuming), and handed him the sheet of paper.

"Um," LePage said, after retrieving his glasses from a table and looking at it.

"At least it's not about politicians," he said, as he blow-dried his hair. "I hate politicians, and I detest stories set in your friendly neighborhood bar. I also abhor stories about people in the television business, including so-called celebrities. But libraries, I have always liked libraries. My mother was a librarian."

Overwhelmed by the positive character of his reaction, Brian decided to have a little coffee, a half a cup black, which he served himself.

"But is this really true?" LePage asked, "that someone in Ohio is actually putting money in books to promote reading?"

"It's a quirky state," said Brian, "as I can attest because I was raised there. In Cleveland, I understand that people are planting all sorts of things in books, even baseball tickets to sold-out games, to promote reading.

"Is that so?" said LePage. "You got to be kidding. I like baseball, and I like the hard-luck Cleveland Indians."

"Elsewhere in the country people are doing the same thing," Brian interjected. "There's a sort of national craze about reading, which is developing even as we speak."

"Is that so?" said LePage. "That's good. I'll run it by some of our public relations people, see what they can do to fan the flames. Meantime, stay in touch. Get your agent to call Stella, and she'll send you a check. Get to work on a pilot script, and assuming this company doesn't collapse in the meantime I'll read it myself before turning it over to the nit-pickers.

"By the way, I forgot to ask how you became acquainted with Stella. She's a nice girl, but what a face."

"Let's save that for next time," suggested Brian, as he headed for the door, light-headed. So giddy that he couldn't resist snarling through the window at the dog in passing the guard tower before he turned out onto the Pacific Coast Highway in the direction of a travel agency to purchase a ticket to Cleveland.

Chapter 6

Book Thief

The news that someone had been apprehended stealing a rare book from the Plymouth library led off the discussion at the July meeting of the Friends Council -- the day before the installation of a computerized catalogue.

"The theft of books has never been much of a problem here," said Louella Winters, commenting on the story in the newspaper. "Of course like libraries elsewhere, we are accustomed to people filching books occasionally, including ones they are too embarrassed to check out, like The Joy of Sex.

"I don't think anyone has ever figured out whether the people who steal books in other categories, like the occult, Satanism, witchcraft, and astrology, are motivated more by a desire to remove them from the shelves, lest they influence malleable young minds, than by a genuine interest in these subjects. The same is true of works on gay and lesbian subjects -- and even on Charles Darwin …."

"Charles Darwin!" interjected Neal Barker, "I can't believe it."

"Neither did I," Louella replied, "until I found out that some Creationist here in Plymouth had removed all the cards from our catalogue referring to Darwin.

"A similar sort of warped compulsion explains why books in which an author has used words that are offensive to the members of some ethnic group, or those espousing some religion or creed, 'grow legs,' as we librarians say. You are familiar with the controversy over the N-word and books by Mark Twain, even Tom Sawyer and Huckleberry Finn.

"In recent years, too, there has been a startling growth in people purloining from our shelves books about, or even touching upon, the subject of abortion."

"And a good thing," said Preston Myers, who was a leader of Plymouth's pro-life movement. "We should have removed those books long ago on our own initiative."

"Please believe me, I did not mean to point the finger at you, Preston," Louella said, defensively.

"Oh, go ahead and point!" said Hawley Short. "But we're not here to discuss Preston or abortion. Tell us about the thief, Louella."

"Yes, I guess it's up to me to describe what happened," Louella said, "as I was in a manner of speaking an eye-witness to the apprehension of the book thief here at the library.

"It happened shortly before the library closed on Friday. I had just finished clearing up a paper jam at the copier when our street person called out, telling me to dial 911 as he raced out the door.

"While I was on the phone, someone at the circulation desk later told me he wrestled to the ground out in front of the library a well-dressed gentleman, and retrieved this," Louella said, holding up a slim book.

"Why, whatever is it?" asked Lydia McGovern. "I should have thought that our library had little worth stealing."

"It is titled 'Return of the Whole Number of Persons within the Several Districts of the United States,' and it is a record of the country's first census in 1790. As you can see it's only 56 pages long," said Louella, "and you're quite right, Lydia. It is one of just a very few books our library owns, which you could characterize as rare."

"Our thief has taste," said Hawley Short. "Who is he?"

"The police have identified him as Charles Stringfellow. Apparently, he comes from a wealthy family in upstate New York and has been identified at the scene of book thefts in several states, including Ohio," said Louella.

"Reminds me of that fellow Stephen Carrier Blumberg of Ottumwa, Iowa," said Hawley, warming up to deliver another monologue. "You may recall that over a 16-year period he stole more than 24,000 volumes, weighing 19 tons, -- rare books and manuscripts from 327 libraries and museums in 45 states and Canada.

"He didn't need to steal, had a trust fund which provided him with $72,000 a year, on which he could have lived handsomely without lifting a finger. He was driven to steal by what they call "Bibliokleptomania," an obsession to have physical possession of books, and the more books and rare manuscripts the better in the judgment of those who suffer from this peculiar affliction.

"When the police raided his home in Ottumwa, they also found a large collection of old stained-glass windows and 50,000 antique brass doorknobs. It seems this Blumberg fellow was trapped in the past, in the Victorian era to be precise about it. His fixation extended even to wearing antique underwear of that period, which he didn't change for weeks on end."

"Well, I don't know what kind of undergarments Stringfellow was wearing," said Louella, laughing. "But he is certainly not in Blumberg's class. In searching his apartment here in Plymouth and his family's home in New York State, the police found only enough in the way of stolen books to charge him with a minor felony. He has, moreover, admitted his guilt and pledged to mend his ways."

"So much for our thief," said Preston Myers. "What does this incident tell us about our street person? Can you shed any light on that, Louella?"

"Not much, I'm afraid, though of course I thanked him for having intervened. He said he had acted out of gratitude for the library's hospitality, and that he would likely be moving on soon.

"Apart from that," Louella continued, "I just want to say that although he still dresses in rags, I suspect him of sneaking off from time to time to take a shower. He sure smells better. I could have sworn that he gave off the scent of cologne the other day, when he was reading a book, a real book."

"How wonderful!" said Lydia McGovern. "Our efforts to promote reading seem to be bearing fruit."

"May I suggest that we place one of your bookplates in a volume to honor our street person for his apprehension of the thief," said Charles Whitney. "It would, of course, be better to have his name. Barring that, I should think that 'street person' would do very nicely."

"Charming idea," said Lydia, "and if you will permit me, I would be so bold as to suggest the perfect volume. It's a recent work called <u>A Gentle Madness</u> by Nicholas Basbanes, an account of the obsession that drives book thieves even as it does such renowned collectors as John Pierpont Morgan, Henry Huntington, and John Carter Brown. There is not all that much difference between the obsessive book collector and the obsessive book thief, according to Basbanes. It's only their methods that are different, and in some instances, as he points out, even that difference is quite slight."

From the subject of theft, the discussion of the Friends Council drifted on to other matters. There was much to catch up on, including how libraries everywhere in Ohio had picked up on Lydia's bookplate idea. In a related development Buckeye veterans' organizations had mounted a statewide campaign to insert patriotic bookplates in the hometown libraries of all those who had served in America's various wars.

"That reminds me," chimed in Lydia, the other night I had a call from the Association of Funeral Directors of America. It seems they want to recommend to funeral home directors that they include a page in the little booklets they pass out to the bereaved, suggesting consideration of a bookplate by way of honoring the deceased.

"The person who called asked if they might use my name on the page, but I declined, saying it would be more appropriate to credit all of us, the Council of the Friends of the Plymouth Public Library. I hope that was all right."

"You are too humble," said Neal Barker, "the credit certainly belongs to you, but I for one am only to happy to share in your glory."

"Hear! Hear!" said Preston Myers, raising his mug in toast. "I only wish there was something stronger than coffee in this porcelain vessel.

"To Lydia! Who has provided a free opportunity for immortality!"

"Unwittingly, you are right, Preston " interjected Hawley Short, "for books have lasted a great deal longer than anything else created by the human hand, as I was reading only the other day. They have outlasted even the crumbling ruins of the libraries in which they were once stored in a good many instances."

Amid much light-hearted banter on subjects relevant and irrelevant that were dear to their hearts, the light faded in the sky, and the members of the Friends Council took their leave. But not before Louella had reminded them that the library would be closed to the public the following day for the installation of the new computerized catalogue.

"Of course, any of you who are free, will be welcome to come and watch."

"Just try to keep us away," said Lydia, who was there with almost all of the others promptly at eight in the morning, when a large white truck painted with the familiar logo of a well-known computer company pulled into the loading dock. Shortly after Eric Motley had turned on the lights and opened the back door, three green-jacketed technicians transported into the building on book carts large boxes stenciled with mysterious markings.

"You'd think we were receiving a shipment of replacement hearts or livers," said Hawley Short, observing the fastidious care with which the technicians handled their cargo. His remark, which was directed at no one in particular, was overheard by Neal Barker.

"Oh, this shipment is more valuable than a mere shipment of ordinary body organs," said Neal. "What we're seeing here is the arrival of a whole new brain for a library that can't go on living without it."

"If you mean a brain for someone who is no longer able to use the one the Almighty gave him, why then I guess I could agree with that."

"Oh, come off it, Hawley," said Barker. "The library you venerate is like some old, superannuated aunt being kept alive by tubes. A vegetable, someone who should hasten to make out a living will so that her meaningless existence can be terminated peacefully. Now, we've got something better, something that will breathe fresh life into the old doll, make her young and vigorous again.

"Think of it -- essentially the same machine that put a man on the moon, that enables us to manufacture more cars with fewer workers, that allows a dairyman to sleep late, confident -- thanks to a computer chip -- that each cow in his herd will be fed a diet perfectly suited to her individual needs in producing more milk, here in our very own Plymouth library.

"It's progress, Hawley! Progress!"

"Thank you for the sermon, brother Neal," Short responded sharply, distraught that for this so-called "momentous occasion" the main reading room had been totally rearranged. Tables previously set aside for reading now accommodated boxes, inside of which were computer workstations.

"No doubt about it, Armageddon is upon us," Hawley Short said, moving away from Neal Barker and toward the old card catalogue that was about to be loaded into the big white truck.

"Where are you taking it?" Lydia McGovern, who was similarly despondent, asked one of the green-jacketed technicians, members of "some new Satanic priestly class," as she believed, presiding at a secular rite that was becoming familiar at libraries around the nation with the arrival of the computer age en route to the creation of what was called "artificial intelligence."

"To the state penitentiary," the technician replied.

"Has it committed some fell offense, then, which merits incarceration?"

"Oh, no," said the humorless technician, anxious to get on with his work. "We just have orders to deliver it there. The warden said they can use it in the prison library."

"Well, there's some good news, at least it's not going to a landfill," said Hawley, who stayed on at the library with Lydia long enough to wave a fond farewell to the catalogue and its beautifully burnished old trays.

Meantime, the technicians unpacked during the course of the morning all the plastic housed components of the new system, and hooked up a welter of cords and cables. To facilitate this process, holes were drilled in the tables to accommodate computer workstations for the use of patrons, which were all wired into the new mechanical contrivance. It was a busy scene. The green-jackets scurried here and there, like an angry swarm of bees, lusting after their queen.

After lunch, when everything was in place, Louella Winters was summoned from her office to watch the next crucial events unfold, as the foremost among the technicians pushed some keys that brought the machinery into operation. With additional prompts from him on a master keyboard, the machine then seemed to take over on its own, in self-congratulatory fashion awarding itself a "PASS" on each in a long series of internal tests of all its various component organs.

Following that, everything was in readiness for the insertion of the patented PROGRAM, which was the invention of highly paid commissars called "programmers," as Hawley Short had learned from Neal Barker. These apparatchiks, apparently, devoted their lifetimes to the arcane pursuit of inventing so-called "software," preferably starting as children of the sort who eschew reading, and even baseball, in favor of playing video games.

By then Hawley Short had returned home to offer his wife a recital of the baleful events, to his way of thinking, which had transpired at the library. Correctly sensing his mood and to cheer his flagging spirits she read aloud the newspaper account of the reopening of the restored old downtown Cleveland Public Library.

"I'll skip the part about how what was supposed to take five years and cost $90 million took more than seven years and cost more than $102.5 million," she said.

"Nothing like Cleveland politics!" snorted her husband.

She read to him instead of the renovated lobby, with its vaulted ceiling, the elegant rooms and coffered ceilings, the walls of Botticino marble and the floors of Travertine marble -- all fully restored to their former splendor, as patrons might have found them in 1925, when Calvin Coolidge was in the White House.

Meantime, in her office Louella read a letter of apology from Charles Stringfellow, delivered by a messenger in livery. "I'm glad I was apprehended," the letter said in part. "I have pleaded guilty, and am expecting shortly to be sentenced to a term of less than two years at the state penitentiary where I expect to be working in the library at the same time that I take a correspondence course in library science offered by Kent State University.

"So from stealing books I shall go to the other side of the table, so to speak, maintaining a collection of them, with little likelihood of theft here in the prison, as I would imagine."

For reasons she would have found it difficult to explain to anyone else, Louella answered the letter immediately, wishing Charles all good luck and a speedy release. Thus began a mutually engaging correspondence between one professional and another en route to becoming a professional.

Chapter 7

MOODEY'S RAGE

Dwight Moodey was in a worse mood than usual when Louella Winters paid a visit to his new quarters in what she knew would be a vain attempt to assuage his hurt feelings. It seemed that with the arrival of the new fax machine, the only place it could be conveniently located was in the little room next to her office, where Moodey, who was in charge of acquiring new materials for the library, had been working for years.

So he had to move out, or rather down, into the basement where he was threatening to raise mushrooms in protest of what he told Louella was both his "literal and figurative descent," though he certainly didn't blame her for it.

No, the process of his "debasement," as he chose to describe it, had begun a long time ago, shortly after he had entered upon his chosen profession. Back then public libraries used to call what they added to their collections "Acquisitions." This meant books and periodicals, and the budget permitting, a few old manuscripts and the like -- materials that could be displayed from time to time to make patrons feel proud of their library.

Over the years, the operable word had become "Items," a catchall term that more accurately, if more vaguely, described what was increasingly housed in buildings still euphemistically called libraries, though increasingly the libraries themselves - particularly those on college campuses - were adopting some alternative name, like learning center. The distinction was not lost on Moodey, who still, anachronistically -- like many of his fellows across the land -- had the title "chief of acquisitions," which he believed a gross misnomer.

This was why he had scrawled indignantly "THE CHIEF OF ITEMS

HAS BEEN REPLACED BY A MACHINE" on the message board of his former domain before carting his belongings to a cramped cubicle in the basement.

Of all the members of the library staff the quirky Moodey was the most-outspoken opponent of the automation of library functions, which he viewed as a dark conspiracy on the part of Satanic corporate America to shackle libraries to its infernal products. To Moodey the computer represented social isolation, confusion, insecurity, and unemployment. In time, he feared, it would eliminate white-collar jobs the way automation had already eliminated blue-collar jobs.

Though he had long ago despaired of successfully resisting the computerization of library functions, Moodey was not about to give up without fighting a delaying action. He was a proud graduate of the library school at Kent State University -- "the last such accredited school that remains in Ohio," as he often reminded people, "which is not surprising as nothing I learned there has the slightest bearing on what I do at the Plymouth library. I would have been better prepared for what I am doing here with a degree in social work."

"I'm truly sorry that I had to consign you to the basement, Dwight," Louella said, as she found Moodey tacking up on the wall of his new abode a quotation from the late-19th century librarian J.Y.W. MacAlister:

"My critics will tell you that the more time-saving apparatus is used the more time the librarian will have to cultivate his intellect and discourse with his readers on the beauties of Browning or of Byron. But is the time saved by mechanism used in this excellent way? I am afraid not. The taste for such things grows on what it feeds, and the librarian who has invented an appliance for supplying his readers with books by means of an automatic ticket-in-the-slot machine will not be happy, or spend any time in reading Browning, until he has invented one which will, by the touching of a button, shoot the book into the reader's home."

"Don't think it's my idea," Louella pleaded with Moodey, whom she considered the most valuable person on her staff. "In Columbus they are insisting that I fax our reports to the library high command. Nor is that the end of it. At our last regional library meeting the powers that be actually pressured us all to acquire cellular phones for our personal automobiles."

Her sympathetic words had their intended effect in calming Moodey's rage. He knew she had not personally betrayed him, that what was going in libraries across America was beyond the power of any single librarian to withstand or repair.

"Don't worry, Louella, I'll be a good soldier."

But he struggled with a deep bout of depression that lasted for weeks. It was not just the machines, but the changes that had overtaken the work he had once loved, which accounted for his dour mood. Formerly, he had taken real pride in pouring over publishers' lists and dealers' catalogues -- proud that to him of all people on the face of the earth was accorded the responsibility of acquiring new books for the library. He had belonged to a vanishing species, agonizing over whether the library should acquire this or that edition, the work of this historian over another, this volume of poetry over hundreds of others, only after having cast a critical eye over dozens of reviews.

Like his fellows -- at least the good ones -- Moodey was an omnivorous reader, reading everything he could get his hands on before reaching his decisions. But over the years this prerequisite of his honorable calling had changed, owing to a combination of factors, which were beyond his control. One was the consolidation within the publishing industry itself that had resulted in fewer and fewer editors deciding on which manuscripts would be published.

Another was a consolidation within the critical review process, brought about by the demise of independent organs of review, including a whole raft of magazines with people on their mastheads called book editors, and the concomitant demise of book reviewing as a special department within the pages of many newspapers, not to mention the elimination altogether of second or alternative newspapers in cities across America.

Moreover, when the newspapers that remained had to cut costs to survive, the axe had always seemed to fall most heavily on book departments. Publishers knew that if they tried to achieve the savings necessary to stay afloat by diminishing other sections, the comics, for example, they would soon be faced with a subscriber revolt.

Yet, there had still remained a glimmer of hope. It flickered in the pages of the weekly Book Review Section of <u>The New York Times</u>, the newspaper of which Adolph S. Ochs, a native of Cincinnati, had gained a controlling interest in 1900. Ochs and his heirs had always been scrupulous to maintain a sharp distinction between what was news and what was something else.

But about the time the term "acquisition" yielded to "item" in library parlance, that distinction was no longer honored where books were concerned. This had happened sometime in the late 1950s by Moodey's reckoning -- he had been unable to pinpoint the exact date -- when the newspaper began distributing its Book Review Section a week in advance of its actual publication date to book-dealers, that they might then have on hand the books people would be buying as a result of reading it.

"Of course that was when we still had book-dealers," as Moodey advised a young woman, in trying to discourage her from following a career like his own. "The numbers of independent bookstores have declined by about half since 1991, leaving only slightly more than three thousand today. In the process their share of the book market has fallen from 33 percent to just 17 percent, with the big chains taking up the slack."

The final desecration of the Book Review Section in The New York Times, Moodey believed, was embodied in the decision to illustrate it with silly caricatures and artwork, thus robbing it of several thousand words of text. But maybe that was not particularly significant, as by then the incestuous relationship between the book industry and the review process had been forged, and the Book Review Section had become essentially an advertising supplement devoted mainly to works written by ghosts for famous people and celebrities.

Or for so-called "Blockbusters," books written by a few heavily-promoted authors, who had achieved "brand name" status thanks less to their literary merit than to skillfully managed programs of public relations. And the book industry -- no longer run by editors but by promotional people and graduates of business schools -- had run amok, providing fewer and fewer opportunities for the Dwight Moodeys of this world to show their stuff.

"But did it make any difference?" Moodey often wondered. For people's tastes by then were molded mostly by what they saw on television or by scanning reviews all flowing from a single critical faculty, the Book Review Section of The New York Times. Because, of course, newspaper publishers elsewhere had found that they could save a lot of money by dispensing altogether with book editors of their own.

Worse yet, there was the growing and strident demand for non-book materials, reels of videotape with movies, CDs with music, and on the horizon the DVDs which were soon to replace videotapes in the public esteem. This left the hapless Moodey perforce pouring over the pages of slick video and music magazines, and pondering whether his title should not be "Chief of Entertainment" instead of "Chief of Items." Nor was he just being facetious, for entertainment was what he had to order to keep his job, in response to patron demand

Meantime, the imperative to acquire new machines was soaking up the lion's share of the library budget anyway, leaving the Moodeys of the world either to commit suicide or be "good soldiers." By then a noble calling had been reduced to allocating what scant money that remained to buy a few fatuous best-sellers, mysteries and travel books, and only very occasionally a reference work -- the latter having become prohibitively expensive in published form, as compared with the cost of buying them on discs for use on computers.

Amid such gloomy thoughts Moodey retrieved his pocket-knife from one of the boxes in which he had moved his possessions.

"I'll be damned if I'll use the electric sharpener," he vowed, as he ran the blade back and forth to put a point on a pencil, before taking a break and repairing, as he often did to comfort himself, to the only place left in the library which remained "unspoiled," though he, like its keeper, knew it was on the "endangered list." This last place of quiet repose and refuge was the Genealogy and Local History Room, which was lodged upstairs and looked very much as it had forty years previously, when Mary Mountfort arrived to head up its collections and activities.

Ranged about the walls of the comfortable though cluttered room, there were oil portraits of Plymouth notables from the past. These included the late head of the city council who had died in the prison to which he was remanded for taking kick-backs on public works projects -- why is it that crooks are so often remembered longer than upright citizens? -- and the black-suited founder of the town, whose portrait was paired with that of his stern-looking wife, similarly attired in black with wisps of pale lace below her high collar and above the heavily-starched cuffs of her dress.

Unlike those downstairs, the few tables in this room still fulfilled the function for which they were crafted, providing space to spread out family charts and documents, though Mary Mountfort was convinced, and Moodey agreed, that when she retired within a few months this would change. Like everywhere else in the library the place would be jammed with machines, and the records that she and a dedicated corps of volunteers maintained in old catalogue trays "com-pu-terror-ized."

Her clientele, mostly people in their late fifties and up, reciprocated the affection Mary had displayed toward them over the years. Unknown to her, some of them -- including the two gray-haired volunteers, fresh from the hairdresser, who were filing away cards when Moodey popped in on his break -- had raised a small purse and commissioned a local artist to paint Mary's portrait in oils, using a photo of her in her prime. In due course Mary's likeness would thus hang on the wall in the company of scoundrels.

Moodey nodded to the volunteers as he sat down for a little chat with Mary Mountfort, who was churning inside over the breakdown of her answering machine.

"It is," as she told Moodey, "absolutely the first and the last machine" she would allow in her domain.

She had purchased it out of her own meager salary when, owing to a budget cut, she had lost her sole, part time assistant, who had been paid a pittance for answering the phone a few hours a day. Feeling it would be a dereliction of duty to miss a single call, Mary Mountfort had installed the answering machine with Neal Barker's help.

When she had returned from the dentist's office that day, its red light was flickering, indicating that someone had called. But when she pushed "PLAY," pencil and paper at the ready because the machine repeated messages only once before erasing them, the infernal contraption emitted a short garbled sound and then jammed.

Fingers trembling, Mary had extracted the little tape cartridge, managed to move the tape a little ahead by inserting the eraser end of a pencil into the rotating little spool in the hope that the tape would become unstuck and divulge its messages. But to no avail. Finally, in desperation, she had unplugged the little monster, and then plugged it in again. While she was bent over the socket in the wall, she heard what sounded like a man's voice.

"But who? I guess I'll never know," she said to Moodey, who commiserated with her.

54

Having observed Mary's anguish out of the corner of her eyes, one of the volunteers filing cards at a table spoke soothingly to her.

"Oh, he'll call again if it's important," she said.

But he didn't, and Mary was tormented by the perfidy of the little machine for the rest of the day, though the next day the gentleman in question showed up in her office shortly before noon, looking well tanned though it was the depth of winter.

"Say, my name is Brian Hedley. I'm working on a little script about a public library about like this one. Is there some place we could talk privately, or better yet would you allow me to take you to lunch?"

"A script," she said, "that sounds like Hollywood."

"It is," said Brian. "It is. Now, how about lunch?"

"If you insist," Mary replied, blushing girlishly. Approaching retirement, she was more than ever a sucker for a good-looking young man. "But first let me plug in this answering machine once more, not that it will do any good."

"It already has," said Brian. "You see I tried to leave a message on it yesterday, but it sounded as if it had jammed. That's why I'm here today."

Chapter 8

B RAXTON

No sooner had Brian Hedley seduced Mary Mountfort in her heavily-scented apartment out on the edge of town -- which had just sort of happened one evening over a glass of wine -- than she was filling his impressionable ears with anecdotes enough for a dozen episodes of his television series. She had a flair for gossip and a cheerful, engaging way of describing the foibles of those who "had found a home," as she put it, at the library.

"You have to remember that a library, generally speaking, is a place where misfits from other walks of life often end up," Mary told him by way of introduction to the subject. "For most of those on our staff, the library represents 'a second chance' -- a place to recover from a previous failure or succession of failures.

"I tell you this, dear heart, by way of explaining why about a third of those who enroll in library school are between 30 and 40 years of age and another third, between 40 and 50. But I won't tell you some of the unbelievable things staffers at the Plymouth library failed at before they came to the library. You'll just have to worm that out of them by yourself."

"Not even a hint?" pleaded Brian.

"No," Mary said firmly, "not even a hint, but I'll divulge everything I know about our patrons. 'Monkeys in clothes,' I call them, ever since that evening I ran into a Baptist minister, masturbating in the stacks."

"Masturbating in the stacks," said Brian incredulously, "you've got to be kidding."

"No, I'm not, though, of course, being a lady I pretended not to notice. Funny thing, he was not even near anything that might be considered erotic. Poor man!"

As the two of them talked, Mary was intrigued to learn that Brian had

56

graduated with a degree in film arts -- "movies," as he called it -- from Bowling Green State University, which was not far from his hometown of Independence, Ohio.

"I didn't know colleges offered degrees in that," she said in astonishment.

"Oh, no, it's quite commonplace," Brian said. "Moreover, Bowling Green has one of the country's most extensive collections of 'Popular Culture,'" a category of materials, Mary said, she was only vaguely aware existed.

"I spent months in the dreary, overcast winter months, holed up in the library, pouring over old comic books and promotional pamphlets on rock and roll stars in that collection," Brian explained. "For my courses I had to watch mostly videos of classic or little-known old movies, or documentaries on the lives of Hollywood celebrities, notable directors and producers -- that sort of thing. It was only rarely that I had to dip into a book or two on which some movie was based or about the history of the cinema to bone up for exams."

"Then you must make up for that while you're here in Plymouth, and start doing some serious reading," Mary scolded playfully, as she put a pot of coffee on the stove and retrieved a bag of cookies from a cabinet, before heading off to the shower. Munching on them, Brian made hasty notes in a little notebook on some of the anecdotes she had provided, which might prove useful in shaping his pilot script.

Following up on Mary's tips, by day Brian ranged about the Plymouth library, soaking up atmosphere and learning how things worked. At her suggestion he invited Dwight Moodey to lunch several days in a row.

"If I have a best friend on the library staff, it's Dwight," Mary had said, "though I should say that he does not have a sexual twinge in his body. But monkish and celibate as he may be, he can explain to you things that I can't. Me, I'm just a girl who can tell you funny or sad stories. But Dwight can fill you in on the bigger picture of what it all means."

Brian found Moodey in his basement cubicle, and, as Mary had predicted, he was not at all bashful in expressing himself.

"What an opportunity you present," he said, on learning of Brian's assignment. "A chance for me to extract a little revenge, assuming what you are working on ever comes to fruition, and I thank you for being so candid as to tell me up front that in the strange world of Los Angeles that

57

you inhabit, there is little likelihood of that happening."

"Let's first walk about a little," Moodey suggested, leading Brian upstairs and to the reading room for what he called "the wide-angle, panoramic view."

"Does it remind you of anything?" Moodey asked, pausing for an answer from Brian, which was not forthcoming.

"In Hollywood terms," Moodey continued, "if I may presume to a knowledge of your profession, which I don't have, we are looking at an episode of M*A*S*H. See the casualties, who are coming in or have come in, all around us -- the homeless, the blind, the hearing-impaired, those confined to wheelchairs -- men, women, and children who no longer read serious or uplifting books but come here for therapy, to entertain themselves. See how that fellow over there is spinning about the revolving racks with videos and best sellers about celebrities in the alcove where we used to keep the reference collections.

"See how patrons and staff members alike are staring at computer screens or browsing the internet -- killing time, distracting themselves from coming to grips with the harsh reality of their wounds. Today's reading room is a sort of fantasy-land, or hospice -- depending on your particular perspective -- created by special effects, for people who suffer from a grievous and very likely terminal disease.

"It was not always this way. We used to deal with readers, people in quest of intellectual nourishment," he continued, "but today the best that could be said of us is that we minister to what you might call 'the walking wounded.' Our library, like those across the land, has become a sort of emergency room or out-patient clinic for the psychologically disturbed, the discards of an age that has taken a really brutal toll on what we still euphemistically call 'the family,' but which, as everybody knows, has become a dysfunctional myth.

"Consider the children, for example. Why do they come to the library? Because mommy and daddy are both off working, an unnatural situation caused by their dedication to consumerism. We are the baby-sitters for both the toddlers and the adolescents, too, as you can see for yourself any afternoon after school lets out, when they come here to hang out. We have become, moreover, and quite literally, a substitute facility for the failed health care system. With thirty million Americans without any sort of health coverage -- or is it more? I can never remember the exact number -- people come here to the Plymouth library to have free check-ups for high blood pressure and tuberculosis. Moreover, we have been drafted for front line service in the wars against drugs and AIDs and on and on the list.

"If you look at it that way, and I do, Louella Winters is our 'Colonel Potter.' The head of our Friends Council, Preston Myers -- he's our 'Major Burns,' and you can fill out the rest of the cast, as you will."

"I guess that makes you 'Hawkeye,'" Brian interjected.

"Well, yes, I guess it does," said Moodey, flashing a rare smile, "and Mary Mountfort, as I suspect you have already learned, is our 'Hotlips Houlihan.'"

Brian Hedley doubled over with laughter as Moodey added, "and here comes our 'Radar.' His name is Neal Barker. He's the only one who seems to have a plausible understanding of what's going on in our M*A*S*H unit. You're in luck because he is going to be talking to some students here today. The penalty is that first you will have to listen to old Eric Motley, our reference person and a man I love though he is demonstrably over the hill and soon to retire.

Moodey introduced Brian to Eric Motley and to Neal Barker. They in turn introduced him to young Braxton Augustus, who had been flourishing under their joint tutelage. The boy, as both Neal and Eric had seen at a glance, was good material.

As he got to know him better, Neal had introduced Braxton to the wonders of computer science, first improving upon his mathematics skills with an ingenious game that the boy enjoyed. Braxton was quick with his fingers, and Neal was soon instructing him in the fine points of Microsoft Word, how a click of the mouse enabled him to check his spelling, how the appearance of a wavy green line under some words on the screen warned that his grammatical construction might be amiss.

By then with Eric Motley's help Braxton had found the newspaper story, describing why Gerald, his Jamaican-born father, had been sent to the state penitentiary. Apparently, laid off from a construction job and in desperation, Gerald had concocted a crazy scheme for robbing the local bank and returning with his family to his island in the sun. But when the teller handed over a paper sack of money sufficient for that purpose it contained a small explosive charge that stained Gerald's fingers with the indelible green that the police found on his hands in apprehending him.

According to the story in the Gazette, he had hoped that the money would provide him with a fresh start in a more familiar and congenial setting.

"Of such are the dreams that many immigrants, like your father, bring to our country," said Neal, when Braxton showed him a copy of the story, "the vision of making some quick bucks, even if it means robbing a bank, and returning to enjoy them at home, where people of color treat other people of color with respect and dignity."

With Eric Motley's help Braxton had re-established contact with his father in prison. Letter followed letter. Motley, who happily supplied the stamps, was interested to learn from Braxton that his father was working in the prison library, shelving and dusting books and answering occasional questions for prisoners.

"That makes two of us," Motley said, when Braxton told him. "Your father and I -- we're both reference men."

With his debt to both Motley and Barker growing larger by the day, Braxton was on hand early to listen to the back-to-back talks they were to make that morning to students from the local high school. Once they had settled down in their seats in the auditorium, Motley rose to address them, to speak of the profession to which he had devoted a lifetime and describe in his customary forthright manner how his work as a reference librarian had changed over the years.

"May I begin," he said, "by saying presumptuously that reference librarians used to be what you might have called 'the keepers of the keys to the library kingdom.' By that I mean that we had special knowledge, obtained through experience, to facilitate intelligent access to our collections of books and periodicals by people like yourselves.

"We knew where what you were looking for was housed in the stacks. We provided advice on how books in the stacks were arranged according to the Dewey Decimal system. We helped you learn how to examine the cards in the catalogue, and look for the little hints that would lead you to additional writings of relevance to the subject you were researching.

"In support of our work the library maintained a large reference collection with books that contained between their covers large compilations of facts in various categories. These reference works used to stand where the

60

videos and best sellers are today.

"Our job was to help people find the right reference books to guide their search for the answers to their questions. I must say I miss those days, when there was time for me to develop a friendly relationship with students like yourselves. Not infrequently I felt useful. Some students were so kind as to acknowledge my helpfulness in the papers they submitted to their teachers.

"Today it's completely different. The reference books are mostly gone, replaced by CD-ROMs, compact discs -- each one capable of storing more information than a whole set of encyclopedias. From helpmate and counselor to those in search of information, I spend more and more of my time simply keeping abreast of all the mechanical changes, which represent progress according to people more learned than myself, who have calculated that a new generation of technology is arriving in the nation's libraries every three years.

"This means that every three years there are things that must be learned and unlearned in keeping up with how to use a library efficiently. The changes are occurring with such startling rapidity that they are like an out-of-control locomotive racing down the track. My job is to throw the right switch as fast as I can, to avoid a calamity. My ability as a reference person is measured today not so much by thoroughness, as it was in the old days, but by my speed.

"If I, who used to consider myself a keeper of the keys to the library kingdom, may make a confession: we have arrived at a moment when the amount of knowledge available at a public library is increasing so fast that it dwarfs the ability of reference people like myself to keep up."

By the time Motley had reached this point in his talk, most of the faces in his audience had glazed over. Particularly those of the seniors in the audience, who for the most part were in the process of wasting a precious year of their young lives experimenting with drugs and sex in a public school system, which had failed utterly to answer the educational needs of their particular age group.

As Motley sat down, there was only a faint trickle of polite applause, mainly in anticipation of the morning's other speaker, whose appearance in the back row as Motley was winding down had sparked considerable interest.

Neal Barker, sharply dressed in an expensive suit of Italian cut, exuded the confidence of an athlete who is in top form as he rose to speak. He was like a sprinter, coming out of a crouch in the blocks and racing off toward the finishing line.

"The reason I'm here," he said, pausing to smile and allow Motley to make his exit, "is to give you the other side of the story, but to understand what I'm going to say, you'll have to first of all WAKE UP!

"Come on, everybody up on his or her feet, time for a seventh inning stretch!"

The students responded to his exhortation with alacrity. The diversion succeeded in creating keen expectation among them as they sat down again in their seats.

"With all due respect for Mr. Motley, I'm here with some good news. Libraries like this one," Barker said, rising up on the toes of his patent-leather shoes for emphasis, "are finished!"

There was a burst of laughter. One of the Black students raised a clenched fist: "Hey, right on, man! I like this!"

His interjection touched off another, more voluble round of laughter and some scattered applause.

With a wave of his hand Barker quieted them down. "I've got even more good news for you," Barker said, nodding toward the student who had raised his fist, "and for other African-Americans, Hispanics or Asians out there -- because in the world in which you are growing up, we're in the majority by a ratio of at least four, and maybe as high as five, to one.

"Let me hasten to add, I intend no offense to those of you who are White. I'm just setting the record straight, laying the cards on the table, you might say.

"And yet this library, like those across this great land of ours, has mostly books by and about White people, beginning with our own planter aristocracy, the so-called founding fathers, like George Washington and Thomas Jefferson and all the rest of the slave-holders.

"The ironical part of my story is that the Whites have overdone it, by writing so many books about themselves that libraries can no longer afford to buy them, much less store them. Consider one example I read about the other day. The Yale University Library had just one thousand books when it opened its doors in the early nineteenth century. By 1938 it had nearly three million books which required 80 miles of shelves and a card catalogue with ten thousand drawers.

"Now, if it keeps on growing at the same rate -- and it is! -- by the year 2040 -- just 40 years from now -- it would require six thousand miles of shelves and three-quarters of a million catalogue drawers to keep track of the two hundred million books Yale would have. It would take eight acres of space just to house the catalogue."

"Wow!" a pretty young Hispanic girl exclaimed.

"Glad I caught your attention," said Barker, flashing a smile at her. "Another funny thing is that serious studies by people with long foreheads indicate that fully half of the books that today's libraries are buying never circulate. Yes, that's true! About half just sit there, gathering dust and taking up shelf space. Nobody is checking them out. Nobody is reading them.

"That figure will grow because, as I said, though Whites are cranking out more and more books about themselves, there are proportionately fewer and fewer White readers.

"Again, no offense intended, just trying to get across the facts."

The students were listening, ears open, on the edge of their chairs, anxiously wondering what he would say next.

"Now THE REALLY GOOD NEWS," said Barker, sensing that he had them in the palms of his two powerful, big hands. "The age of the computer has arrived just in time to save us all. It represents our only chance to get a handle on the situation, to get a fresh start, if I may say so.

"Consider, for example, the computerized catalogue we have installed here at the Plymouth library. Its capacity is practically limitless. How much space does it require? A few square feet.

"But that's just the tip of the proverbial iceberg. Why keep a bulky set of encyclopedias on the shelves, when all you need is a disc that holds everything in those twenty or thirty volumes in a tiny fraction of the space? When you can find out on your screen whatever it is you want to know from an encyclopedia with the click of a mouse or by pushing a couple of buttons?

"Now I don't want to confuse you or overload your brains, but you are all familiar with video discs, the kind you check out with your favorite movies. A single video disc can store about a thousand books with five hundred pages each. Again, if you want to read one of the books, a click of the mouse, and you have it. And in no time at all, you'll be able to print out a copy for yourself, to read at home.

"They used to call the library 'mankind's memory.' Well now, thanks to the computer, that memory has become infinite. As the technology improves, it is becoming possible to store more and more information in less and less space. The day is already here when people are installing computer terminals in their homes, on which they can tap into that enormous reservoir of information at the library without even putting on a hat or coat.

"My message to you today is: become part of it, the information society. Admission is free! Don't walk, run! Run away from the past and toward the future. Reach out! Find out how the computing machines work, and you'll never want for a job. And I'd like to talk about that maybe another day, as we've run out of time."

These final words precipitated a burst of sustained applause. The students were on their feet. So was Brian Hedley, who made a beeline for Barker to book an appointment for an interview.

"This is pretty exciting stuff," he said. "I'd like to know more about it for the script I'm working on."

When Louella Winters poked her head in the door, she could feel the electricity in the air as she worked her way toward Barker, who was surrounded by students.

"You've done it again, Neal," she said, pumping his hand.

"It's the subject, Louella. I get carried away. It's a good thing I wasn't born a cannibal. You remember that story about the cannibal family that sat down to dinner?"

"No, I'm afraid not," said Louella.

"One of the children said: 'But I don't like grandmother,' and the mother replied, 'Then please just eat your vegetables.'"

"Which reminds me," said Barker, taking Braxton Augustus by the hand, "I promised this young fellow some lunch."

At the local malt shop, the two of them discussed plans for the visit Neal had arranged to take Braxton to visit his father in jail the following weekend.

"I'll be there for you promptly at 8:30 a.m. next Saturday, old man," said Neal. "It'll take us a couple of hours to get there, and if the weather cooperates we'll put the top down on my convertible."

"Sounds swell," said Braxton.

"By the way," Neal continued, "the warden said your father is a model inmate, doing a great job in the prison library, and even taking some correspondence courses in library work at Kent State University. The warden also said your father is a shoo-in for an early release when the parole board meets in a couple of months."

"Yeah, he wrote me about that," Braxton said, smiling. "Now can I say something I shouldn't?"

"Sure, you know me," Neal replied, leaning over the table, all ears.

"Well, I don't know how to tell you this," said Braxton, "but I sort of liked what Mr. Motley said at the library this morning. What you said kind of, well - it kind of scared me."

"I can understand that," said Neal, "and I am certainly proud of you for being man enough to tell me that right to my face. I guess in defending myself, not that I think what I said needs defending, the best I can do is say that it's a frightening world out there. But just because of that one can't just throw in the sponge and give up. You got to keep at it, trusting that in the end things will work out all right.

"Now, how about a slice of apple pie?"

Chapter 9

PRISON LIBRARY

Louella Winters had told herself that she would not go a block out of her way to see him. But in mapping out her trip to the regional library convention in Columbus, why there it was, smack dab on the route by which she planned to return -- the State Penitentiary where Charles Stringfellow was serving a two-year sentence for stealing books.

She was happy that she had decided to pay him a visit as she took the turn off the main highway. It would help to clear her head, which was still spinning from the frantic pace of the long weekend's activities. Three days and nights crammed with exhibits and noise, and shrill pitch-people -- the carefully prepped representatives of an array of commercial enterprises devoted to profiting from what Vice President Gore had tagged "The Information Age," or was it "The Information Highway?" -- she could never remember which.

In preparation for that day corporate America had already, long ago, thoroughly perverted the original purpose that had brought together librarians from around the state. This was to provide an opportunity to get to know each other, compare notes on common problems, learn from each other's experiences, and hear about possible jobs that might be of interest.

In bygone days the libraries by rotation had hosted such affairs on their own premises, proud of a chance to show off their collections of special merit. Louella could still remember the professional purity of those annual get-togethers shortly after she had become the director of the Plymouth library -- when there was still an unwritten rule against any hint of commercialization.

This tacit injunction was first violated when the librarians had opened their doors to the display of a few harmless novelties, microfiche cards and their readers, for example, which saved space devoted to storing bulky

66

telephone directories and the like, in return for small corporate donations to their state association. There had followed displays of electric typewriters, whose makers again donated some money to the group's coffers.

Back in those days, it seemed no harm was being done, as the products displayed were useful and their cost was not such as to break any library's budget. But with the passage of time that had changed by ever larger and larger incremental steps. A well-known publishing house with some unsold best-sellers on its hands, for example, had generously offered to host a reception at which there were real drinks and mouth-watering hors d'oeuvres -- a cut above the gallon of grocery-store wine, the block of Kraft cheddar, and Nabisco crackers that the library association had been able to afford on its own.

Thereafter, the timing of this reception, which was jointly hosted by several publishers, had become among the most important considerations of the committee that planned the agenda for the annual meetings. It must fall not too early in the proceedings to offset the natural anticipation of its occurrence, for free drinks with black Jack Daniels bourbon and Beefeater gin were then -- and still are -- something of a rarity in library circles!

The impact of the affair was not lost on other publishers, whose books are commonly found on library shelves. They worked out their own parallel agenda, offering a series of smart, complimentary cocktail hours every evening, while quietly exerting pressure on their fellows from the hotel industry to provide more suitable venues. In time these had become progressively larger resort hotels in the off season, with Olympic-sized swimming pools and hot tubs. There was, of course, a special price for participants in the library meetings, which always worked out to be exactly the maximum allowable per diem amount allowed each librarian for overnight accommodations on library business.

The pleasure palaces were equipped with display halls where vendors could show to advantage a myriad of copiers, audio-visual devices, apparatuses for viewing videotapes or accommodating CD-ROMS -- the read-only discs that contained a welter of information on a mind-boggling array of subjects -- and mount demonstrations of the marvels of hypertext. The latter meant, librarians were informed, the arrangement of text in non-linear fashion, or in other words not as an author intended it from beginning to end, but according to any conceptual scheme whatsoever that a library patron might wish to impose upon it.

In short order the complexity of all the gadgets advertised as essential for the modern library proved intimidating if not baffling to librarians in light of what they had learned in library school. This was, to enumerate the list, how to acquire books and periodicals, how to catalogue them in accordance with the Dewey and Library of Congress systems of classification, how to store them on the shelves, and how to lend them.

The finer points of these seemingly mundane subjects had provided the lion's share of the agenda at the earlier annual gatherings of regional librarians, which Louella attended. In recent years, however, the presentation of papers on such pristine subjects had given way to increasingly arcane demonstrations involving the use of the technological innovations displayed in the cavernous, but well-lighted halls.

Initially, the preponderance of these machines was designed to help librarians determine how well they were doing in serving their various constituencies There were, for example, machines that could tabulate the number of times a particular book had been checked out in any given year or since its acquisition.

The presentations about these machines, which, it was pointed out, would help libraries to compile statistics on the performance of the books they were buying, were often illustrated with slides or filmstrips. These were generally of short duration, thereby freeing up a maximum amount of time for librarians to browse the increasingly vast exhibit halls, and ponder the purchase for their libraries of things they did not understand. Leisure, too, for librarians to listen to cleverly programmed videos or participate in hands-on, inter-active demonstrations conducted by well-tailored sales representatives from the companies which produced all the gadgets.

"We must innovate, we must abandon our obsession with print, and we must reposition ourselves on the growth curve of the electronic information cycle," said one such rep, to whom Louella had listened at the recent meeting. In introducing an expensively appointed exhibit, this same young man had the gall to snicker in recalling how he, too, had once been a librarian, before warning his listeners of what he called "ominous threats to their tenure owing to the emergence of 'the information marketplace.'" By this he said he meant "threats from competitors who are making information available for profit, and delivering it to more and more homes via cable -- the same cables that provide cable television."

Such nonsense was still subliminally spinning through Louella's head as she reached the guardhouse at the state penitentiary, where a crisply uniformed police officer checked her name against the day's visitor list and provided her with a visitor's badge. After parking her car, she walked to the entrance, where a trusted inmate, who was soon to be released, met her with a broad smile.

"My name is Gerald Augustus," he said. "I'm Braxton's father."

"Say no more," Louella interrupted, raising her hand. "Braxton is a favorite of everybody at the Plymouth library."

"That's so nice to hear from you," said Gerald, as he escorted Louella up to the prison library. "By the way, I wonder if I could ask you please to thank Neal Barker for bringing him here for a visit. We had a lot to catch up on."

Once they reached the library Gerald excused himself, and Louella turned her attention to the man she had come to see.

"When I explained to the warden who you were, he gave me special permission to meet you here, in our library," said Charles Stringfellow, who looked the aristocrat he was, even in prison stripes.

"How do you like it?" he asked, anxiously awaiting her reply.

"Oh!" she said, smiling in awe. "Just give me a moment to take it all in."

While Charles sat down in his chair behind his desk, Louella turned slowly full circle around on her graceful legs.

"If I had a hat," she said, "I would throw it in the air, like Mary Tyler Moore."

For there, as Louella beheld with a rush of joy, all spread out around her, was exactly the kind of library she had known as a girl. There was a series of about a dozen freestanding stacks, which supported with their sturdy arms several thousand books. The sunshine, pouring through tall windows on the far side of the chamber, bathed the room in natural light through slender bars in stripes perpendicular to those on Charles's prison suit.

The beautifully weathered oak tables with green-shaded lamps and real light bulbs -- not the fluorescent ones that flickered over the tables in the Plymouth library -- had ashtrays.

"Why Charles," she said, enviously, "you are not allowed to smoke here, are you?"

"And why not? As a matter of fact I rather like to smoke myself. Will you join me?" he asked, holding out a silver cigarette case.

"Don't mind if I do," Louella said, in wonderment that there was still a library in the United States where smoking -- which is such an agreeable accompaniment to reading a good book -- was permitted.

Charles had no sooner lit her cigarette than Louella, seized by girlish desire, blew a smoke ring, and he laughed.

Sensing her delight, he noted that most of the books in the library were castoffs from public libraries or had been donated by relatives or friends of prisoners.

"There are so many people who donate books," he said, 'that we are considering the formation of a group, like your friends of the library, to support our acquisitions program.

"As you might imagine, this prison, where it costs about as much to incarcerate someone as it would to send him to Harvard, has little in the way of a budget to buy books. Most of the equipment we have here was discarded by libraries elsewhere in the state, which the prison acquired merely for the cost of transporting it."

"Truly beautiful," gushed Louella. "It reminds me of the first library I used to patronize when I was a small girl. Why look there! You even still have a card catalogue, like the one we used to have in Plymouth."

"Yes, and there is no wonder that it may look familiar to you," said Charles, "because it was donated by your library when you installed a computerized catalogue -- just about the time that I was stealing your books."

"Is that so?" said Louella with delight in her voice. "But what's most impressive of all to me," she continued, "is what this library doesn't have. I don't see a single computer or copying machine, or fax, and on and on the list might go."

"Well, that may be changing shortly…," said Charles.

"Oh, don't say that," interjected Louella.

Sensing that what he was about to add might upset her, Charles changed the subject.

Nodding appreciatively, she turned to admire his handsome face, guessing, intuitively, as she sat down, that he had something on his mind.

"I wanted you here for a very special reason," he said, looking deeply

70

into her intelligent eyes -- the smoke from their cigarettes forming a single plume, as it curled up toward the high ceiling.

Louella found his intense gaze pleasing, and she responded in kind, looking deeply, too, into his eyes.

"You see I've just learned that the parole board is going to give me an early release. More than anything else, I'd like to celebrate that with you, my release I mean, in Plymouth if that's possible."

Louella could not conceal a pretty blush, nor the sudden rush of an out-of-the-ordinary sort of feeling for this particular inmate.

"You see, by then I'm hoping to have lined up a job that I would hope to be qualified for, though I could certainly use some help from you."

Wondering what he might be getting at but confident that he would tell her all in his own good time, Louella basked in his considerate attention. As the hour of her visit flew by, they talked of many things, of catalogues and shelf lists, of inter-library loans and a hundred other matters that used to occupy librarians, when they were still in complete control of their noble and self-sacrificing profession.

When she finally took her leave, she did so reluctantly with a firm, congratulatory handshake and a smile, and experiencing a kind of inner womanly joy.

On the drive back to Plymouth that feeling sublimated the nightmare dread of new technology that had been re-awakened at the regional meeting in Columbus. But when she reached the outskirts of Plymouth, she emerged from a very pleasant interlude of reverie to face an unpleasant reality.

The statistics she would soon be compiling in the days ahead for the library's annual report would confirm once again that in Plymouth, as in communities across the land, people were foregoing the pleasures of reading in favor of watching videos or listening to music recorded on compact discs.

"That's the glum truth of the matter," she told Hawley Short, "except in prison libraries, like the one where our book thief is working."

"That's wonderful news," said Hawley, "that Stringfellow has found himself among books he can't possibly steal. Not to mention the role Ohio prisons have played historically in nourishing good writers. You may recall that William Sydney Porter, better known to readers by the pen name

O. Henry, wrote some of his best short stories, perfected his craft you might say, in the old Ohio Penitentiary in Columbus, when he was incarcerated there shortly before the turn of the last century."

C HILDREN

"Now there, young fellow," said Hawley Short, bending to comfort a small boy, the source of the ear-piercing sound he had heard from the circulation desk where he was checking out some books.

"What did you say your name was?"

"I didn't!" said the tearful youngster, wiping his eyes with the handkerchief Short produced from his pocket.

"Well, then, I'm asking you now. Let's have it," said Short. "Jasper," said the boy, "Jasper Bickford."

"Now then, Jasper, or if you prefer, Master Bickford. Whatever it is that you desire, that you shall have. I assure you of that, as surely as my name is Hawley Short, and you may call me Hawley."

By then one of the volunteers in the children's room, where the incident occurred, a woman of experience in such matters, had reached the scene. With a remarkable economy of words -- her work of helping to sort out the grievances of children in an age when they are bombarded with violence on television allowing little time to dally -- she elicited from Jasper the cause of his outburst.

It seemed that young Jasper had his heart set on being a Power Ranger that day, but the suits to enable him to look like such a fierce warrior had run out owing to heavy demand. In the brief interval that it took the volunteer to explain this to Hawley, a second young boy in the children's room began sobbing. Unfortunately, neither Hawley nor the volunteer could figure out what this youngster wanted, for he spoke only Spanish.

Fortunately, María Álvarez appeared on the scene at that precise juncture, and was able to elicit from this youngster, Pedro Martinez, that he, too, wanted to be a Power Ranger.

Apprised of this, Hawley had a suggestion: "María, let's you and I team up. If this good lady will indicate the direction to an establishment purveying such get-ups," he continued with a nod to the volunteer, "I'll gladly supply transportation and money to buy them in exchange for your company." And with that, these two friends of the Plymouth library sped off on one of the innumerable errands that are indispensable to the operation of any children's room today.

"Well, María," said Hawley, as he settled down behind the steering wheel, "Jasper and Pedro have provided us opportunity for a chat, and the chance to perform a small service for two of the library's most prized patrons.

"But I must confess, on learning about Power Rangers from that helpful woman, I couldn't help but think how much the children's room has changed of late. You certainly don't remember, María, but when I was growing up there was no children's room at all."

"No children's room!" Maria expostulated incredulously. "Why whatever did the library do about children?"

"Well, nothing very special," Hawley continued. "When I was a youngster, children were simply patrons like everybody else, young and old alike. There were, to be sure, a few low-ish stacks set aside for what were called 'juvenile materials.'

"When I was a boy, children generally visited the library in the company of one of their parents. Their parents, I should add most emphatically, did not just dump their kids there, as they do today

"For children back then visits to the library were considered rather special treats. They had a civilizing effect on youngsters. Visiting a library for them was a sort of rite of passage, the prelude to something like a bar mitzvah -- an initiation, if you will, into the mysteries of manhood. The children themselves were well washed and scrubbed and fed, I hasten to add, before heading off to the library.

"Moreover, we were not allowed to check out books on our own until we had come of a certain age. Until that moment arrived, our selection of books was carefully guided and monitored by our parents on whose library cards they were charged out. That, it goes without saying, was in the days before television, when reading aloud was still a common practice in many, if not most, homes, certainly in mine. That meant that the quality of the books we checked out back then was much higher than those the children of today take home, as no right-minded parent was about to expend the necessary energy to read aloud from something trashy."

"Sounds utopian," said María.

"Well, I'm not trying to exaggerate and make it sound better than it was, and of course I realize that feelings of nostalgia sometimes overwhelm objectivity. But when that era passed, we lost something valuable, I think, the intellectual bonding that took place early in life between children and their parents, the library playing the role of facilitator. But here I am going on and on and boring you, when I would much rather listen to you."

"You remind me, Hawley," María said, "I told you once that the first time I visited a library I simply wanted to wash my hands. I remember it as if it were yesterday. We knew very little English. We had been working a very long and hot day in August, picking tomatoes and cucumbers, starting before dawn. One evening on returning to the migrant labor camp after dark, we saw a library off in the distance. It looked so inviting, its lights glowing in the still and pitch black, and I asked my father if we might stop.

"Imagine our surprise to learn that we were welcome there and permitted to use the restrooms. I remember vividly the warm clear water, how good it felt to wash off the dirt caked on my arms. While I was waiting for my parents, the librarian explained to me - she spoke a little Spanish -- that we could borrow some books, if we liked, on a free temporary card.

"With her help I borrowed El Pequeño Príncipe ("The Little Prince"). Even though it was quite late after my mother had made our dinner, she read from it to me before I went to bed and showed me the pictures."

María went on to describe how, subsequently, her family had borrowed some records, including a couple on learning English for Spanish-speakers, which they played on an old phonograph player someone had left behind in the camp.

"That's why I am so ashamed!" said María, suddenly dissolving into tears as they pulled to the curb in front of the shop purveying Power Ranger paraphernalia.

"Ashamed? Why whatever for, dear girl?" he asked, turning toward her.

"Ashamed at how I yelled at that street person in the library. What right had I, María Álvarez, a girl who first visited a Gringo library to wash her hands, to scold someone like him? Or anyone?"

"Sounds like a confession, when it would seem to me, not being a priest, a confession is entirely unnecessary," said Hawley. "Now dry your eyes," which Maria did on the same handkerchief Jasper had used.

"You know," said Hawley, "I'm glad you mentioned the street person. Ever since he apprehended that fellow who was stealing one of our books, I have been wondering what he is really up to.

"Dwight Moodey said he saw him somewhere out on the edge of town, entering a nondescript office building to which he appeared to have the key.

"Louella Winters said she'd swear she had a fleeting glimpse of our street person down in Columbus, though he was dressed in a conventional business suit.

"Charles Whitney says he cashed a sizeable cashier's check for him at the bank."

"All very interesting," said María, pushing up her glasses on her nose.

"Yes, it is," said Hawley. "There is definitely more to him than meets the eye."

"All the more reason for me to be ashamed of the way I treated him," said María, as the tears welled up in her eyes again.

"Not the way I see it," said Hawley. "He's the one who should be apologetic for the false colors he is apparently flying."

After Hawley had purchased the Power Ranger suits, which he thought were outrageously expensive given their flimsiness of their construction in some sweatshop of Communist China, the two of them made their way back to the library. Where they were rewarded by the broad smiles of two grateful boys, who happily donned the weird-looking costumes.

María stayed on for a while to read aloud in Spanish from El Pequeño Príncipe to young Pedro Martínez, who soon had forgotten all about his grievance before the magic of the story. It was a remarkable demonstration of the power of a good book.

Hawley, meantime, returned to check out the books he had left at the circulation desk where he could not help overhearing a group of irate mothers demanding of Louella Winters that the library schedule more in the way of children's activities. They had set the stage for their visit by sending a flurry of letters to the editor of the Gazette in advertisement of their main grievance. This was that the Plymouth Library was falling behind others in the region in its purchases of video games and children's videos for home use. The same letters also suggested longer and more varied children's programs and the construction of a Ronald McDonald playhouse for birthday parties.

The irate moms had also suggested that the library break new ground "get with it," was the way they put it -- and enter into an arrangement with some local fast-food establishment to provide a full Saturday lunch for youngsters. This should include pizza and hamburgers -- "something they like" -- in supplement of the juice and cookies the library regularly served in the mornings and afternoons. Such a welcome change, the moms pointed out, would enable parents to leave their children at the library all day long, and obviate the necessity of preparing something for them to eat at mid-day.

Suffice it to say that Louella, who listened with utmost courtesy, had heard it all before. Indeed of all the many special interest groups that lobby the libraries of America, none is more strident than the parents of America. This had become particularly marked in recent years, when most of their numbers are in the workplace, and when more and more of them have become single moms or single dads, frantic to find a place where they can park the kids.

By definition, libraries are universally considered "good for children," and today's mothers and fathers look to them to play an increasingly important role in the nurture of their youngsters. Nor is the number of parents who are of this opinion dominated by those who are on welfare. To the contrary, parents who make the most demands on libraries predominantly belong to the middle and upper-middle classes, and view the free facilities of a public library as something of a well-justified offset to the material assistance provided through welfare programs to the poor.

As Louella sought to extricate herself from the importuning of this particular group of moms, she let drop something she wished she hadn't. "If you'll excuse me, I have an appointment with someone from Hollywood."

"Hollywood?" the moms repeated in a chorus. "Hollywood!"

But by then Louella had vanished and closed tightly the door of her office where Brian Hedley was waiting.

"I wanted to thank you first for all the hospitality," he said, rising from his chair. "I have really enjoyed talking to all the people here. My assignment is going pretty well. You know when I started it, I was afraid there might not be enough color in a library to make it all work. But that has proven not to be the case at all.

"Still, it's a challenge, no doubt about that, cutting through all the stereotypes about libraries as sort of sleepy places served by dull librarians. It's no wonder that not much has been written about them. They're both such complicated subjects, difficult to handle.

"The man for whom I am writing a script is working on a strategy to change that, to use the power of public relations to enhance people's understanding of libraries. At the moment he's trying to drum up interest on the part of some of the talk shows in having some of your people as guests.

"From his standpoint the more talk shows they appear on the more we can reach people and create interest in the pilot episode of 'The Friends of the Library,' and beyond that interest in the show as a series.

"This leads me to ask: who do you think could do the best job of getting the ball rolling, articulating the nature of libraries to a mass audience?"

"That's a difficult question," said Louella, "there are so many angles to it. But why not begin where all the publicity began in the first place with the member of our Friends Council, named Hawley Short, who put ten dollar bills in books. He was our Minuteman, so to speak. He fired the shot, which seems to have reverberated around the nation."

"Good idea," said Brian, making a note of the name.

While he was doing so Louella added: "if I may make another suggestion, you must really visit a prison library some day. I've just recently returned from the one where the thief, who was apprehended stealing a book from our library, is serving his sentence. It was quite an eye-opener, to learn that people behind bars are among our country's most avid readers."

Chapter 11

TALK SHOWS

It was not long before Hawley Short had his brief brush with celebrity, as a guest on local radio and television shows. "My last chance to be outrageous," he said to Lydia McGovern following his debut performance, "to badger listeners and viewers about getting out to the library and reading some books.

"That's my 'stump speech,'" he added with a smile, "delivered while sitting on a chair that felt like one, a stump that is."

Matters of personal comfort aside, Hawley thoroughly enjoyed himself, appearing live and uninhibited in the homes of thousands of people. There was opportunity for him to talk and talk about libraries, the most arcane details of their operation, and to "air" -- literally -- his pet theories about an assortment of topics.

"I have yet to achieve my ambition of publishing a novel," he told Mrs. Short over morning coffee following one of his appearances, "but appearing on the idiot box goes a long way toward making up for it. Imagine all those people out there in viewerdom, with nothing better to do than listen to the opinions of yours truly, and watch me scratch my nose."

"Yes, I have been meaning to say something about that," said Mrs. Short. "It's difficult sometimes for me, and I suppose for other people, who are watching, too, to tell whether you are scratching it or picking it."

"Well, maybe a little of each," said Hawley, with a wry grin. "It may interest to you to learn, as I did just the other day from a delightful elderly lady from Oberlin, that the average person fingers his or her nose 60 times every day. That works out to slightly more than four times every waking hour, though I don't know whether or not that figure includes scratches. I neglected to ask her."

"Then just maybe you ought to try to do something about it," said Mrs.

Short, as her husband headed out the door en route to Cleveland for an appearance on the Julie Leslie Show, a program on the local arts and entertainment network. Following his introduction, he wasted little time in lambasting TV, the medium he blamed for the decline in reading. "With all due respect Julie, and I probably shouldn't be saying this as an invited guest in your home, so to speak, but television is like quick-sand," he said, winking at the camera, "a treacherous place to set foot."

While the studio audience was tittering over the audacity of his opening thrust, Short reached into the pocket of his worn horsehair jacket and pulled out a clipping, which he waved in front of the camera. "But just let me read to you from this," he said, leaning forward in his chair toward Julie. "It's a story about how reputable experts are warning that many of today's health problems are caused by our inability to open the windows in public buildings …."

"What has that to do with reading and books, our subject for the day?" Julie interrupted, still smarting from his barb about television.

"You'll see in a moment," Hawley retorted, raising his hand for silence.

"You see most of our libraries are all sealed up. There's no fresh air!" Short exclaimed. "According to this article, a company in Missouri has figured out a way of inserting rotating wheels into the exterior walls of these buildings to facilitate an exchange of the stale air inside with the fresh air outside.

"But my question is: why not just fix it so that you can again open up the windows?" he asked to a ripple of laughter and scattered applause from the audience. "That would at once help to prevent the spread of contagious diseases -- the drizzlies and drippies passed around by the staff and patrons at our public library in Plymouth during the winter -- because the windows are shut up tight from the outside world in the interest of economizing on the heating bill. A false economy!" Short snorted, banging his hand on the little table in the TV studio and rattling the coffee cups.

After the show was over, Julie, whose sang-froid was well known to tens of thousands of her fans, thought that it had been an unmitigated disaster. Until she looked in her mailbag and E-mail file and found that viewers in unprecedented numbers had communicated their agreement with Short. Many of them expressed the hope that her show would revisit "this important subject" in the future.

80

Following that appearance Hawley ran into Lydia McGovern again. "I have to tell you, dear Lydia, that my experience of television has confirmed entirely my worst suspicions. It is a nit-wit medium. But here's a flicker of hope," he said, showing her an invitation to appear on the Ted Chandler Book Hour.

For his first appearance on this prestigious show, which was nationally syndicated and watched by many librarians, Mrs. Short insisted that he get a haircut at a pricey, single-sex barbershop in Plymouth, a place Hawley had not previously set foot.

"And please ask the barber to trim the hair in your nose," she said. "I have been thinking that perhaps that's why you scratch it so often."

Hawley did as commanded, though it tickled when the barber trimmed around his schnozzle, and it pained him to pay more than twice as much as he usually did for his bi-monthly shearing at a place that offered a ten-percent discount for seniors like himself.

But it was worth the exorbitant price, he had decided, when Ted's make-up girl complimented him on his fresh cut, as she patted on cold cream to take the shine off his pink cheeks before the show. Once the ON AIR red light flashed, and following Ted's introduction of "this stalwart friend of the Plymouth, Ohio, public library, who has fired the first shot in a national revolution in reading," Hawley launched into a description of the Dewey Decimal classification scheme.

"I urge everybody watching this program to become familiar with the name of Melvil Dewey," he said, "an Amherst College graduate who back in 1876 devised the scheme for classifying books, which is still in use by most public libraries around the nation today."

"When you say 'classifying books,'" Chandler interjected, "could you just explain that for our viewers?"

"Be delighted to," said Short. "By classifying books I am referring to the system for arranging them on the library's shelves -- to facilitate their storage and retrieval -- so that you can find them when you want to read them."

As the studio audience dozed off, Short then explained, with as much sparkle as he could bring to a tedious subject, how Dewey had subdivided books into a series of ten numbered categories, beginning with 000-099 for general works, "encyclopedias and the like," and ending with 900-999, books on history and geography, that sort of thing."

But he could see that he was losing the interest of the audience, and very likely those out there in viewerdom, as well. So he rushed through his explanation of how a mere hundred numbers had proved inadequate to accommodate all those in each category on the ordinary public library's shelves. How the ten categories, therefore, had been further subdivided, and how finally resort had been made to the use of a decimal point followed by further numbers to keep pace with the human race's ever-expanding store of knowledge.

"If you're looking for books on useful insects, for example, the number is 638, books on beekeeping 638.1. books on silkworms 638.2, and so on," he said, as Chandler fidgeted in his chair, and the audience did likewise.

"But let me tell you," he said "about how the librarian of the Plymouth library, Louella Winters, put the kibosh on the defacement of the walls in the Plymouth library's lavatories. This, she had done," he said as the audience reacted with interest, "by the simple expedient of affixing large sheets of newsprint with duct tape on the walls of each stall and inviting library patrons, who were so disposed, to scrawl their thoughts while seated on the commode.

"For example," Hawley said, reaching behind his chair for the fresh roll of such scribbles he had brought along, as Chandler winced and hurriedly signaled for a commercial break.

Back on the air Hawley, having heard from Chandler, had replaced the roll of newsprint behind his chair. "Ted asked that I not show you these samples of what people are writing on the walls at our library lest they offend your sensibilities.

"But permit me just to add in conclusion on this subject that one of the sociologists at our local college is actually supplying the newsprint now, free of charge. He's paying for it out of the grant he received from the federal government in Washington to write a study on -- and here I am quoting -- 'The Sociological Implications of Writings on the Rest Room Walls at the Plymouth Public Library.'"

Moreover, Hawley affirmed, as the audience laughed heartily, "when the news of this scholar's project was published in our newspaper, it spurred an immediate burst of creativity on the part of people using the library's restrooms. I suspect a good many people of 'using' the facilities just for an opportunity to express themselves, if you get what I mean."

Chandler winced again, as the show -- mercifully from his perspective -- was running out of time amid sustained laughter and cries of "More! More!"

Upon returning home Hawley was exhausted and moreover vexed, as he told his wife, at the studio audience's reaction to the Dewey Decimal system. "They were bored out of their gourds," he said, "but, aha, focus the light of wisdom on what people are writing on bathroom walls, and it's quite a different matter entirely. Ted told me that it was one of the most popular segments he has ever aired. The show was scarcely over when his sponsors were calling to insist that he run it again and again in future promotional advertisements of his program."

In a subsequent appearance on the Ted Chandler Book Hour, Hawley had people across the nation gnashing their teeth when he described how Louella Winters had been forced to eliminate the position of a woman -- "we'll call her Samantha" -- who had previously answered the telephone in the librarian's office.

"To balance the budget and in the name of so-called 'progress,'" Hawley explained, "Samantha was replaced by an answering machine and a recorded message with a lot of information callers don't want to hear, before connecting them with someone on the library's staff if the caller knows that person's correct extension.

"Otherwise, the phone just rings and rings until someone at the circulation desk, which is often a very busy place, picks it up.

"Samantha's removal from her accustomed post had worked a special hardship on elderly patrons of the library," Hawley continued. "They had enjoyed chatting with her, as indeed did people of all ages, who wanted to complain about something."

To replace the latter void, he explained, "Louella put up a special bulletin board, called 'ASK THE LIBRARIAN,' on which patrons were invited to make known their grievances, anonymously, on Post-its supplied by the library.

"I don't think Louella ever leaves the library at the end of the day without having added a Post-it of her own to each and every Post-it complaint, fully explaining the library's position vis-à-vis the original Post-it, no matter how insulting or arcane.

"And sometimes there are Post-its to her Post-its, and on and on, until the matter, no matter how unimportant, is finally laid to rest."

This had proved popular among almost all of the library patrons, who got a laugh out of some of the more strident demands and Louella's answers, Short added.

"Here is a typical example," Short said, holding it up and reading: "Dear Librarian -- Someone is always working the daily puzzle in The Plain Dealer before I get a chance at it."

"In her Post-it to this Post-it, Louella promised to make a copy of the crossword for safekeeping at the circulation desk before putting the paper out on the rack, but no one showed up to claim it.

"After waiting a suitable interval, Louella then attached a Post-it to her earlier Post-it, asking simply 'Well?'

In due course there appeared yet another Post-it saying: "Too embarrassed to ask," which proved the end of the matter.

"During the winter, as you might imagine," Hawley continued, "there are always numerous complaints about heating and lighting."

"Like most of the rest of the world we have to use fluorescent bulbs for reasons of economy," Louella had Post-ited someone complaining about the latter.

In her answer to one about the lack of heat in the 900 stacks, Louella had snapped: "I don't know why it is, but people who read history seem to have a low metabolism. The heat in those stacks is exactly the same as in those housing books on religion. Is it that faith will keep you warm? I don't know. But I suggest to the history complainer: why not wear a sweater?"

With more and more people tuning in to catch the latest words of Hawley Short, "THE TALKING HEAD FROM PLYMOUTH," as he was billed in the ads placed in TV guides by his own anonymous backers out in Hollywood, Short soon found himself appearing on "WHAT'S MY GRIPE" show, a weekly show hosted by the popular Phil Warner. There, he derived immense satisfaction from exacting his personal revenge on the book publishing industry, which had become largely, he said, "a lady of the night, spreading her legs for anything that might bring in a buck."

"Can you illustrate this with an example?" asked Phil, pleased by the provocative tone of his guest's opening sally.

"Well, just consider the category of biography," said Short. "The

84

computerized catalogue at our local college in Plymouth yields a list of 5,541 books on Adolf Hitler. Even subtracting a few for duplicates or translations and re-editions, that, by my calculation, adds up to about one hundred books a year on the Führer, author of the Holocaust. And what new facts do the vast majority of them contain?

"Practically none!" he exclaimed, as the studio audience roared with approval.

"The situation as regards Hitler is so out of hand that I personally favor a national law that would license new books on him to, say, ten a year -- the same way hunters and anglers are limited to so many ducks or fish a day during the season in the interest of preserving the species. In the case of books, the goal, of course, would be to preserve a dwindling supply of library space for something worthwhile.

"Moreover, what is true of Hitler is also true of more than a half dozen World War II generals. At present, for example, there are more than 800 books on Douglas A. MacArthur, which are endlessly, hopelessly repetitive. What possible purpose would be served by 800 more? Or by adding to the more than 400 books each on Patton and Rommel? I say enough already. They should be covered by the same national law. We should limit the number of new books on all three of the aforementioned generals to, say, five a year, with the understanding that anybody who wants to write about them can do so, by winning one of the licenses in some sort of a national competition."

Hawley's suggestion sparked vigorous debate in pages of a literary magazine, which ran a lengthy essay titled "We Don't Want To Forget About The Holocaust, But I Could Do Without Another Book On The Führer." Several writers of letters to the editor subsequently agreed with the author, though a spokesperson for the American Civil Liberties Union threatened a retaliatory lawsuit in protection of the First Amendment guarantee of free speech.

But few people - almost nobody, as a matter of fact -- quarreled with Short, when he availed himself of an appearance on the Fox network to say: "The library is the last bastion of decency in America. Everything else has been corrupted -- the political system, the banks, once admired corporations, even a good many religions -- including even Christianity, as witness the number of unsavory televangelists who have been revealed to be not only corrupt, but immoral.

"But when was the last time you read a story about a corrupt or immoral librarian? It is a profession that attracts honest, decent people. There's something about working in a library that has a cleansing effect on people, and, if I might add, a certain rich humility, too.

"The rewards are not great. When was the last time you heard of a rich librarian?

"And that precisely is one of the dangers. For the people who make and repair the machines on which today's library depend are very well compensated indeed. A copying machine repairman earns well in excess of the average librarian, the makers and sellers of the copiers much more.

"This has created a disturbing imbalance in the system, which is not an argument for paying librarians more, because pay is not what attracted them to their profession in the first place. In this, they are not like your average doctor, who could not possibly have attended a medical school without learning that his was a high-paying profession.

"Nor is this an argument for returning to the past. The present is here. The future will be dominated by computing machines and the internet. During my lifetime the only comparable experience of such a revolution in technology was the invention of television. Remember how, initially, there were such high hopes for this new medium -- dreams of using television to eradicate illiteracy, globally, and how those hopes were dashed to the point that to turn on the TV set in a classroom today would be to subject pupils to an unremitting diet of sex and violence.

"It is my considered opinion, by the way, that it doesn't matter how much we spend on education, our children will continue to get failing grades in character as long as they watch what they are watching on this idiot box.

"Television, where our children are concerned, has proved a national disaster of the first magnitude. I speak out today in the hope of alerting people to a similar menace posed by the computing machine, insofar as our public libraries are concerned."

While Hawley was rambling on in this particular appearance, the lights on telephones in the studio flashed impatiently, each flash a person calling in with a comment or question.

FIRST CALLER: "What can the average person do about it?"

86

HAWLEY SHORT: "Think about it, buy a copy of good book and read it and when you're finished with it, give it to another friend of a library, and when that friend has read it, have him give it to a library."

SECOND CALLER: "I have a comment. If you ever run for elective office, I'll vote for you."

HAWLEY SHORT: "That's very flattering. But in Ohio we have a very low opinion of politicians, so much so that the entry of someone's son or daughter into that unsavory profession is cause for commiseration. And at my age I am unwilling to be either ignoble or commiserated over."

FOURTH CALLER: "When you get excited I notice that you scratch your nose. Or are you picking it?"

HAWLEY SHORT: "I suggest you talk to my wife. She has the same question."

His answer prompted a request for an interview from a show-biz magazine. When it appeared the magazine ran a caricature of Short, scratching his nose above the caption: "POPULAR TALKING HEAD SAYS HE'S SCRATCHING HIS NOSE NOT PICKING IT."

"There it is!" Hawley said when he showed it to his wife, "my definitive answer to your question.

"But here's a happier note," he continued, reading from the lead-in to the interview: "From Poughkeepsie to Peoria, from Bangor to Nome, friends of libraries are going out to do what Hawley Short is appealing to them to do -- reading is on the upswing all around America."

"And isn't this funny?" he said, reading to Mrs. Short about a lady in Seattle, who had left a sizeable bequest to her local library to purchase 'worthy books about cats.'"

The sum total of many such amusing or bizarre actions, as reported in the press, created a national groundswell of support for libraries and reading of sufficient proportions that Peter Riding, the popular evening news anchor, dispatched a television crew to the Plymouth library for a sound byte. When it was broadcast as the "Event of the Week" tailpiece for his Friday program, Riding said something flippant about the national library craze, before he aired the film strip of members of the Friends Council of the Plymouth Library, chanting in unison: "TURN THIS OFF AND READ A BOOK!"

"Well, as that is the end of our show," Riding quipped, "may I just say why not? -- it's okay with me."

Following that broadcast and another surge in television coverage of libraries across America, Neal Barker found himself in demand as a talk show guest. His appearances were underwritten by the advertising of corporations, anxious to profit from the sales of their machines and software to institutions, which had become hooked upon them, like hypochondriacs on the purple pill.

In one of his appearances Barker, fresh from organizing his own business, Computer Systems Unlimited, showed off his company's multicolored new Greater Access Library Card which, as he explained, patrons could use at any branch of the Cleveland or Cuyahoga County Public Library systems.

"And here's something else that may be of interest," he continued, showing off a portable E-book reader. "It weighs just two pounds, less than a good many single, hard-cover novels, and yet it is capable of storing 100 books. People borrow it from the library for reading in bed."

In an appearance on the Money Hour, Barker described how "for the special benefit of insomniacs," as he put it, the Cleveland Public Library had become the first in the nation to offer internet users a 24-hour-a-day online reference service. "You have only to check into the Library's web-site," he continued by way of explanation. "Library staff people man the reference service during the day. After that, from 9 in the evening to 9 in the morning your questions are answered by the company in Maryland which has devised this amazing system."

Meantime, another member of the Plymouth Friends Council, Lydia McGovern, stepped into the media spotlight as the spokesperson for what had become a national movement to promote bookplates. "The Chamber of Commerce in a fairly sizeable city," she noted in one appearance, "has gone to the expense of underwriting the cost of bookplates in memory of all those who die locally."

Lydia had the studio audience in tears when she read aloud from some of the thank-you notes from the friends and family of those so honored.

In an interesting twist, one public television station devoted a half-hour-long feature to Lydia's life-long hobby of collecting museum postcards of paintings in which artists depicted books. The station had gone to considerable expense to photograph several of the original art works portrayed in the postcards, which were from collections around the world, and hired the noted art therapist, Shandor Magyarsky, to analyze the psychological impact that artists had attempted to achieve through the portrayal of books in their paintings.

"Zeese," Magyarsky said in heavily-accented Hungarian-English of the books in paintings "generally fee-gaire in ar-tees-tick works of art as sim-bowls of serenity, to create an air of calm, ee-ven placidity." Magyarsky went on to describe the manifold applications he had found for books as portrayed by artists in his own recondite practice to relieve stress and anxiety, as Lydia McGovern sat in front of the camera by his side, mystified by what he was talking about.

Thanks to all the publicity about libraries his minions had helped generate, out in Malibu, California, Vance LePage was finding the raising the money for the Friends of the Library project surprisingly easy. The merest mention of the word library seemed pleasing to the ears of prospective financial backers and advertisers. When he coupled his pitch to them with a reference to how his own mother had been a librarian, the money men were impressed.

"Then you must really have your heart in this, Vance," said one of them, "but are you sure you want to shoot the series in Ohio?"

"Well, it's a fairly cheap place to work," Vance replied. "You may have forgotten that Bob Hope was raised in Cleveland. He's promised to put in a couple of cameo appearances if this thing gets off the ground, and he's still on his pins. So has Tim Conway -- he's from a place called Chagrin Falls, not far from Cleveland. And don't forget about Jack Paar. He's originally from Canton, Ohio. Maybe we can prevail upon him to cry a little, like he used to do on the Tonight Show."

Chapter 12

COMPUTER DOWN

On entering the library in the months following the installation of the new computerized catalogue, Louella Winters, who disliked flying and avoided it whenever possible, felt like a nervous passenger boarding a jet airplane. And when the screen on the mechanical catalogue at the library turned a wavy blue, or failed to operate at all, she felt, as she imagined, like a hapless traveler aboard a doomed airliner, whose panicked frame of mind we know from cockpit recordings recovered from the wreckage.

When she confided her fears to Neal Barker -- and that she had begun to take prescription tranquilizers to assuage her constant anxiety over a possible computer crash -- he was sympathetic.

"At least you are aware of your problem and are doing something about it," he said. "That makes you very unusual. Most people are still blithely unaware that we are all of us on this flight into the future, and that it has passed the point of no return. There is simply not enough gas left on board, so to speak, to return to our point of origin.

"So we just have to grin and bear it, and if I may be so bold as to suggest, place our trust in the Almighty, who is our pilot on this journey."

Despite Neal's reassuring words, Louella remained at a heightened sense of alert on the job, her eyes peeled and her ears cocked for any sign of an impending computer failure or glitch at the workstation in her office, which she kept permanently on.

In time, under normal operating circumstances, she managed to mask her computer anxiety most of the time, and maintain a stiff upper lip in the presence of patrons and library staff alike, even as privately her stomach churned lest something go wrong. Whenever this became unbearable she turned for relief to the anti-depressant -- the first prescription medicine

90

she had ever taken regularly in her life.

"I know how you feel about drugs," she told Hawley Short, when he happened to see her popping one. "I heard you on that talk show. But believe me, these pills are a necessity. I just couldn't get through the day without them."

"Well, I'm willing to make an exception in your case, dear girl," he said. "Perhaps, the medical profession should approve that particular nostrum for over the counter use by all who share your profession in this day of the computerized catalogue."

"I don't know about the medical profession," said Louella, "but I have already recommended them to several members of the staff, who share my computer fright."

Meantime, as Neal Barker had suggested, Louella muttered a little prayer each morning on waking, just before switching on the coffee maker: "Please God, make the computerized catalogue work today!" She had just concluded saying that to herself on a day in mid-May when she was seized by a fearful premonition and rummaged in her closet for her running shoes. She would need them, she knew, even if the computerized catalogue were working faultlessly, for this was one of the busiest days of the year. The library would be bursting with high school students bent on hastily completing their term papers, preparatory to taking their final exams.

On entering the main reading room Louella, her shoes laced tight, was thus ready for the worst, and she would not be disappointed. For the main reading room already looked like a zoo at feeding-time. Hordes of students crowded every nook and cranny. As the surfaces of the old tables were taken up by computer workstations, they had covered the floor with their paraphernalia -- notebooks, backpacks, boogie boxes, bags of potato chips and barely concealed bottles of Gatorade in defiance of the sign at the entrance, "NO FOOD OR BEVERAGES PERMITTED IN THE LIBRARY."

It was only with difficulty that Louella threaded her way to her office. En route, she paused to help a distraught student clear a jam at one of the copying machines -- an omen of things to come.

On reaching her office her worst fear was realized. There was an urgent summons to the circulation desk.

"It's happened again!" a young woman at the desk said. "The computer has crashed! What should we do?"

Louella didn't know. But she knew from a glance at the erratically flashing lights on the computer keyboard that it would require a call to a technician.

"Here," she said, trying to maintain some semblance of calm as students impatiently queued up to check out books, "Here's a yellow pad. Just have them put down their names and telephone numbers, the title and call numbers of the books they are taking out. I'll call the computer people."

Louella then sprinted to her office. She popped several tranquilizers as she dialed and redialed a number again and again, to busy signals, before, finally, getting through to a recorded message: "YOUR CALL IS TERRIBLY IMPORTANT TO US. IF YOU WILL PLEASE LEAVE YOUR NAME, THE DATE, TIME AND YOUR PHONE NUMBER, AND A BRIEF REASON FOR YOUR CALL AFTER THE BEEP, WE'LL GET BACK TO YOU AS SOON AS POSSIBLE."

Louella's message was succinct: "Here at the Plymouth Public Library we have a computer meltdown. We'd appreciate it if you got here at once! And I do mean at once!"

After hanging up Louella responded to a furious knocking at her door by a small fist.

"Come on in and just leave it open," she called out.

Whereupon a little knot of anxious-looking children burst in. "The key to the bathroom. It's lost," one of them said.

While retrieving a duplicate for them from a hiding place behind the circulation desk, Louella's eye was drawn to a spool of microfilm that was rolling merrily across the reading room floor from the microfilm reader, where a student smirked and watched with delight as it unraveled.

Eric Motley, for the moment forgetting his age, raced to the scene, but too late to prevent the student, who had been mocked by his peers for unraveling one spool, from reaching into a drawer of microfilm and firing a half a dozen more into the air.

"Children, children! This is a library," Motley shouted.

Sheepishly, the student began to repair the damage of his own making.

Meanwhile, in her office, Louella had found that the screen on her own computer had gone berserk. "BOOT ERROR, BOOT ERROR," it flashed.

Pondering the meaning of this weird message, she was suddenly startled by the sound of the alarm at the main library door, a horrendous, ear-splitting buzzing. The noise was triggered when one of the students attempted to exit the building with the books he had checked out, which the attendant behind the circulation desk had been unable to desensitize owing to the computer breakdown, and a heavy metal bar had struck him in the groin.

"Got me! Right in the nuts!" shouted the student, who was wearing an athletic P for Plymouth on his sweater, for the amusement of his mates who quickly pointed accusatory fingers in his direction.

"There's a button behind the circulation desk," Eric Motley cried out, in an absolutely futile attempt to make himself heard above the din.

And it was only after Motley had depressed the button himself, that the strident buzzing noise subsided.

By then Dwight Moodey, grinning from ear to ear, had appeared at the top of the stairs leading up from his basement cubicle. "I've got to say I like it, Louella," he said, surveying the pandemonium with satisfaction. "Reminds me of <u>The War of the Worlds</u>.

"Let's don't get 'em fixed, the machines I mean."

Louella responded with a look of utter exasperation before saying in a low voice, "there is something I wanted to talk to you about," and pointed in the direction of her office.

"Anything at all," said Moodey, following her quick footsteps.

"Well, then, let's begin by closing the door," she said, as the two of them took chairs on opposite sides of her desk, which was piled high with papers.

"I'd like to share a little information with you about our street person," Louella said.

"I'm all ears," said Dwight, perking up and bending closer to catch her every word, when there was an insistent knocking at the door.

The knocker was an elderly lady, a frequent patron of the library, who was dying to tell someone what she had seen in her backyard, though that was not how she began.

"I am truly sorry if I am interrupting, but I would very much like to see someone about ordering a particular book I've heard about."

"Would you mind, Dwight?" Louella asked, explaining to the woman that he was in charge of the library's acquisitions.

"We'll continue our conversation later," Louella called out to him, as Moodey, feigning the attitude of a gallant courtier, escorted the lady out of the door. Upon reaching what he good-naturedly told her was "The Descent" down the stairs into the basement, he placed her arm firmly in his.

"Why, I don't believe I have ever been down here before," she said, enjoying the firm pressure of his arm on hers and already having forgotten the title of the book she wanted the library to order, if indeed she had ever had one in mind.

Like many other elderly people, she lived alone, craved company and someone in whom to confide what she referred to in her isolated existence as "the day's news."

She had discovered that the people at the library were always very friendly, agreeable and responsive to old folks like herself.

Once Moodey had settled her in the only other chair in his cramped cubicle, and ascertained that she couldn't remember the name or indeed the author of the book she wanted, even what it was about. "How stupid of me," she said, rummaging in vain in her pocketbook, "I was sure that I had written it down somewhere. But where?"

"Well, when you find it, you now know where to find me," said Moodey, obligingly. "Now, is there anything else on your mind? Or what's left of it?" he joshed, quickly establishing a kidding relationship with a patron who accepted his jibe with elderly relish.

"Well, yes there is, young man," she said, anxious to share a puzzling event in her day. "It's about the strange thing that happened at my home this morning. You see I had parked my car - my neighbors tell me I shouldn't really be driving at all," she said, blushing, "in the backyard. And this bright red cardinal began flittering about, just above the rear vision mirror on the driver's side. He was doing what they call on the Nature television programs 'a mating dance' -- you know what I mean? Imagine right above the mirror. And...."

She paused to catch her breath, "going squirt! squirt! squirt!

"And, of course, as soon as he had flown off, I went right out with a rag and wiped it off."

"Stop!" interjected Moodey, raising his arm, like a policeman at an

94

intersection, "I have an explanation for you."

"Oh, I had hoped you would," said the lady, subsiding back in her chair and listening intently.

"You see," said Moodey, who was delighted to clear up the mystery, "the male cardinal is, of course, red. But in your rear vision mirror he saw a reflection of himself which was not red, and which he therefore mistook for a female. And so, for reasons of the season of the year -- the birds and the bees and all that -- he decided to mate with the reflection of himself in your mirror."

The woman was entirely satisfied with his explanation, and smiled broadly as Moodey leaned back and laughed heartily.

"You have made my day," he said, "and now, if you please, I would like to show you my mushrooms."

The lady was enchanted by the progress of his little garden in a dark corner of the basement, and after she had gone, for the rest of the day Moodey, could be heard saying aloud: "Squirt! Squirt! Squirt!" to the puzzlement of his co-workers.

When one of them asked him why, he merely shrugged his shoulders and said, "all I'll tell you is that it's about cardinals."

"The St. Louis baseball team?"

"No," said Moodey emphatically, standing, bending his arms at the elbows, and hopping around like a bird, as he reveled in all the confusion in the main reading room.

This included, as he discovered on one of his frequent trips upstairs to take it all in, the sight of old Eric Motley being badgered by a stout gentleman wearing green slacks and a Hawaiian sports shirt. His complaint was that he had taken a coupon from the box where patrons put those snipped out of newspapers that were excess to their needs. It was only upon reaching the cashier at the supermarket he learned that the aforementioned coupon had expired, meaning that he had to pay full price for three bars of soap, which he didn't particularly want.

"It would seem like the simplest thing in the world for this tax-supported institution," he raged with scorn, "to go through the coupons in the box every day and throw out those that have expired."

After hearing him out, Motley had a suggestion. Perhaps the gentleman himself would like to undertake this job.

"Would I get paid for it?" the gentleman asked.

It was only then, Motley's demeanor having well expressed his reaction to this outlandish question, that the gentleman, realizing what an ass he had made of himself, marched out the door, passing in transit a salesman hell-bent for Louella's office.

"But we already have plastic jackets which we use on books that are frequently circulated," she told him. "But to tell you the truth I sometimes wonder why we go to the bother. Everybody takes them off when they reach home. They make the books feel slimy, your hands clammy when you're trying to read yourself to sleep."

"That's just it," the salesman persisted. "We now have a new kind that is non-removable -- can't take them off without tearing off the cover entirely."

"Horrors!" Louella exclaimed, as she escorted him to the door.

Chapter 13

Booksale

Louella Winters was bursting with news, something she desperately wanted to share with the members of the Friends Council at their August meeting. But she bit her lip and waited until they had all settled around the table and ceased talking to spring her surprise.

"I am extremely pleased to announce," she said, clearing her throat and lifting up her chin, "that we have enlisted a volunteer who has expressed his willingness to work on the fall book sale for a month full-time. He will oversee the collection of the books, the sorting of them, and all of the hundred and one tasks that a sale involves, that is, if you will accept his services."

"Is there a catch to this?" asked Preston Myers. "Only a lunatic would make such an offer. Louella, come clean with us. What have you got up your sleeve?"

"Why Preston, whatever in the world could you be thinking of little old me?" said Louella, playfully.

"Okay, let's have it straight," Myers persevered, "Who is he? What loony bin did he escape from?"

"I can do better than that," said Louella, "if María will kindly open the door."

There was a moment of silence.

When María opened the door to the corridor, she let out a squeal of delight, for there in front of her was a familiar young man, clean shaven, hair combed, dressed in well-pressed slacks, sports jacket, and highly polished shoes."

"Mother of God!" she exclaimed, as the street person sauntered into the room smiling broadly and saying: "You may have noticed that I have been here at the library quite a lot over the past four or five months. It's about time I did something to repay your hospitality."

"But how?"

"But why?"

"If that doesn't beat the devil?" were among the surprised interjections and interrogatories that filled the room, as Preston Myers rose to conduct the handsome young man to his own seat at the head of the table.

"On this occasion, this is where you should sit, my boy. We're all ears."

Somewhat flustered by all the attention the newcomer asked: "Where should I begin?"

"How about with your name?" suggested Charles Whitney.

"My name is Larry Higgins. I am a private detective, specializing in what you might call 'cultural cases' -- the theft of precious works of art, rare books, archaeological treasures, that sort of thing.

"I was hired to investigate this library by certain publishing companies in New York City, which I would rather not name to preserve their confidentiality. They asked me to look into 'the strange things happening at the Plymouth Public Library,' as they put it.

"By that the publishers meant, of course, the baffling discovery of dollar bills in books, something they had never heard of before. They wanted to know what books the dollars had been placed in, and whether it was the work of some nut?"

"Well, certainly, there's no secret about that," said Hawley Short. "It was a nut all right. Me!"

"I thought I could finish up my investigation in a few days," Larry continued. "But that proved impossible. The thing unfolded into a story first of state-wide, then of national significance."

In workmanlike fashion Larry Higgins reviewed the events as he had reported them previously to his employers, beginning with Hawley's ten, one-dollar bills.

"By the way, Hawley, if I may presume to call you by your first name, one of the publishers expressed an interest in having a look at the novel you are writing."

"It's okay with me, if it's okay with the Missus," said Short, noting that she was the final authority in their home as to all matters literary. It was she who had, in fact, urged him to throw away all of his previous attempts at writing novels, he pointed out: "Very wise decision, too, if I do say so

98

myself."

Higgins went on to describe how at the request of one publishing house he had himself hidden twenty-dollar bills in James Thurber's books in Columbus. "Seemed a bargain to the publisher, really, considering the high cost of advertising, a cheap way to rekindle interest in a first-rate author. Newspapers in New York devoted considerable space to the story. The New Yorker even led off its 'Talk of the Town' by suggesting that twenty dollars seemed a paltry amount, given the seminal role Thurber had played in the magazine's history. Some of the other publishers asked me to do the same thing, and help revive interest in writers lamentably overlooked by readers today, including some of your favorites, Hawley."

At the same time, Higgins said, he was appalled by the way promoters of all sorts of things unrelated to reading had tried to squeeze onto the bandwagon, planting discount coupons for everything from pizza to movie tickets. He was infuriated that unscrupulous big-box stores had hired youths to put flyers advertising Disney products in children's books. "Coupons for toys and video games," which as Higgins emphasized, "are far afield from the spirit of Hawley's original idea, and some of those several of you have initiated subsequently.

"On a brighter note," he continued, "I am pleased to say that Lydia McGovern's idea on building support for libraries through commemorative bookplates has been copied by hundreds of libraries.

"Moreover, Neal Barker, please tell that bright young fellow you are mentoring, Braxton, that your ideas on promoting computer literacy are just taking off. I have heard there are going to be hearings down in Columbus soon about the feasibility of using state-wide lotteries to promote reading and computer literacy."

"State lotteries?" Barker interrupted, "You've got to be kidding."

"No I'm not. Honestly, that's what I have heard from a very reliable source," affirmed Higgins. "You better get ready to explain to the state of Ohio's elected officials how they might go about drafting legislation to put it into effect."

There was a brief pause as the members of the Friends Council reacted in disbelief.

"Finally, I think everyone around this table can take a certain amount of satisfaction at the way your actions have helped spark a renewed interest in local libraries across America. According to my employers, who have been tracking this thing in their own interest, newspapers, magazines, and television have printed or aired more information on libraries in the previous year than in all of American history, beginning with the founding of the Republic.

"Today, right after this meeting, I'm going to write my final report to the publishers. Then, as I am due some vacation, I thought I'd just spend it in a nice town like Plymouth. And what better way than by helping with the library's coming book sale, that is if you are willing to have me, now that you know who I am and why I have been here."

There was a round of assenting nods and expressions of wonderment around the table as Higgins concluded his breathtaking recital of events. Their heads giddy with all the good news, members of the council got up to stretch their legs, replenish their coffee mugs, and shake Larry's hand or clap him on the back.

When they were all settled back in their chairs Hawley Short observed: "Capable as you obviously are, Mr. Larry Higgins, I'm here to tell you that you'll be needing some help in getting ready for the sale, and here and now I'd like to volunteer the services of María Álvarez."

Turning to her Hawley added in a pleading tone of voice: "María, you always do such a nice job of working out the refreshments."

Though she blushed, María's auburn eyes flashed, and those around the table feared the hot-blooded fury of which she was capable on certain occasions, as during her original encounter with the street person.

"I truly appreciate the compliment, Hawley. But I am entirely capable of speaking for myself, and I'd just like to say that it would be a pleasure."

"Then that's settled," said Louella, as everyone sighed with relief. "The first Saturday in September. That gives Larry and María about a month to get it all together."

Following some discussion of further details, the meeting broke up. Larry Higgins discreetly intercepted María just outside the main door on the front steps, to ask whether he might take her to dinner to make amends for his deceit in feigning to be a street person, and to discuss plans for the sale. Thereafter, he went to the small, unmarked cubicle of an office which he had rented on the outskirts of town, and with the help of a word processor and the several pads of notes he had made in the guise of street

100

person wrote his final report to his employers, the publishers in New York.

In his covering letter he noted that seldom had he enjoyed an assignment so much, that in lieu of a promised bonus he would appreciate it if they would donate copies of books from their current lists to the sale at the Plymouth library, which, he noted, "would draw many curious people from a large surrounding area." In due course the publishing houses responded generously, providing both books and bonus for an assignment well handled.

In the meantime, romance blossomed in the Plymouth library to the immense satisfaction of all who knew about it, which was everybody, as it seemed. It began in the basement, not far from the prying eyes of Dwight Moodey, where María and Larry, dressed in jeans and T-shirts, met in the late afternoons after she finished work to plan the book sale. Together they stacked the books, magazines, records, cassette tapes, CDs, and miscellaneous other items which had been donated by library patrons or were arriving via motorcycle, as the leather-jackets made good on their pledge to Hawley Short.

"I can't tell you what a pleasure it is having intelligent life down here," Moodey told them on seeing them bent to their dusty labor the first day. "Remind me to tell you about the lady and the cardinal sometime. Meanwhile, would you like to see the mushrooms I'm growing? I talk to them every once and a while, and would feel flattered if you would do likewise. It seems to make them taste better."

When preparations for the book sale moved upstairs, it was Hawley Short's turn, on frequent visits to the library, to take an interest in the blossoming affection for one another displayed by María and Larry.

"It reminds me of the old days," he told his wife, who had firmly told him that it was "none of his business," but hung on his every word about it. "Do you remember how a young lad, researching the letter S for Shakespeare in the card catalogue, might well strike up a harmless acquaintance with a young lass of about the same age, who was looking up Shaker, the English sect which practiced communal living and celibacy.

"In the stacks there was no such need to reconcile such differences in interest as prelude to a possible romantic attachment thanks to the Dewey Decimal or Library of Congress arrangement of the books on the shelves. The aforementioned young lass and lad might bump into a soul mate effortlessly, owing to a shared predilection for the poetry of Cervantes, Hungarian cooking, or the history of the Mexican revolution."

"Well, I guess I'd have to say you are right about that," said Mrs. Short, "at least based on our own experience."

"Ah, yes, love in the stacks. What was it we both were researching?"

"You know perfectly well, Hawley Short," replied his wife. "If you have forgotten, I'd appreciate your bringing me the rolling pin."

"No need for that, my sugar cube. It was Petrarch, wasn't it? It was not until our third date that we both admitted that our reason for wanting to read his Canzoniere was to see if our professor was right, that Petrarch, in describing his passion for Laura, never once described any physical attribute of her but her eyes. And yet never to my knowledge does the reader form such a detailed, mental image of a breathtakingly gorgeous woman. I felt as though I would recognize her instantly, should she pass me on the street."

"Yes, and you might just recall that her first name was Laura, which reminds me to ask you sometime why you never use my first name in that novel you are writing."

"Ah, yes," said Hawley, abruptly changing the subject to the mixed feelings they both shared about the impending book sale. Like a diminishing number of people in America who truly love books, they looked upon the news that a public library, any public library and especially their own, was discarding treasures that would not be replaced, as a cause of profound sadness. It was like the bereavement occasioned by the passing of a friend, the demolition of some fine old structure to make way for a drug store, the conversion of productive farmlands into a site for some ghastly new condo development.

This feeling was offset only partially by their anticipation, even excitement, at the prospect of carrying forward their personal crusade, saving as many publications as possible against all reason. For every nook and cranny of their modest home was filled with books. Books! Books! Everywhere! They had long ago given up the race to keep up with them.

There were floor to ceiling bookshelves in every room, including the kitchen and bathroom, which were all filled to utter and complete capacity. In most rooms, too, there were free-standing books shelves, as there were in their double garage where it was no longer possible to park even one car. This was not to mention a category they called "current reading," the piles of books on tables, which were occasionally toppled in the middle of the night by their soft-footed cat.

These facts of their book-crowded existence notwithstanding, the Shorts were nonetheless determined to rise to the occasion once again, as they had many times before, and save as many books as humanly possible. That thought uppermost In their minds, they went early to the book sale at the Plymouth library with their standard equipment, which consisted of two large fold-up carts and several sturdy large bags.

Once at the sale they surveyed the scene with practiced eyes. Their attention was immediately drawn to a category of books they called "artifacts." These comprised mostly works published in the late nineteenth century, which had colorful, incised covers. In no time Mrs. Short had found two of them: an 1899 edition of Louisa M. Alcott's An Old-Fashioned Girl, which was adorned with embossed flowers and gold leafing on the cover; and an 1884 treatise entitled Domestic Problems: Work and Culture in the Household by Mrs. A.M. Diaz. Mrs. Short particularly liked the cheerful scene on the cover, showing two women happily cooking on an old cast iron stove in a large friendly kitchen, half-hidden by an embossed folding screen with a floral pattern.

By the time that she had delivered her standard lament to the volunteer behind a table -- "How in the world can our library part with a treasure like this?" -- Hawley had finished his own first sweep for books in the same category.

"Already found some goodies, eh?" he said to her with a squeal of delight, as around about them small children, clutching their allowances in chubby hands, pored over illustrated books on short-legged tables arrayed with colorful offerings. Their parents, meantime, veered off to the non-fiction and fiction tables where the Shorts had just purchased nearly everything from the last century, solely on the basis of cover design.

"Can't have too many copies of this!" Hawley exulted, showing his wife an early edition of Jack London's The Call of the Wild, which he had purchased for a dime. Its spine and cover were illustrated in bas-relief with a man behind a dog sled, in color.

"See you later!" he said, as he sped off for a "little look-see" in another area of the sale. In no time at all he was moved to save a twelve-volume set of books, entitled <u>The Library of Historic Characters and Famous Events of All Nations and Ages</u> published in 1900. This work's principal compiler, as he was pleased to discover, was none other than A.R. Spofford, called to the job of Librarian of Congress from the Buckeye State. The frontispiece, a marvelous engraving, showed him "Among His Books," according to the caption. There were other engravings of people and events scattered through the volumes, which in Short's estimation made it well worth the three dollars he laid out for the whole set.

As there was now little or no space remaining in his cart, Hawley had to forego buying one of his favorite reference sets, two volumes that he felt no library anywhere should ever part with. This was entitled <u>A Guide to the Study of the United States of America</u>, with well over a thousand pages. Published in 1960 at a price of just seven dollars, it was prepared over many years by two devoted and highly intelligent Library of Congress employees, Donald H. Mugridge and Blanche P. McCrum, who completed the work under the direction of Roy P. Basler, a Lincoln scholar and one of the outstanding directors of that institution's reference legions.

Mugridge and McCrum, known as M & M to their circle of admirers, had summarized thousands upon thousands of books therein described in annotations that are a model of that form. As he was himself among those in awe of their labor, Hawley paused to scan the contents pages of the volume, neatly subdivided into sections on literature and language, literary history and criticism, biography and autobiography, the American Indian, population, immigration and minorities, entertainment, sports and recreation, folklore, folk music, folk art, land and agriculture, and books and libraries, among others. The book was a point of beginning for everything worth knowing about books by American authors published through 1955, with a second and slimmer volume, a supplement, later published bringing the story through 1965,

But as there was emphatically no space for them in his cart, Hawley steered toward a table groaning under the weight of discarded long-playing records with which he thought to fill in the nooks and crannies of his load. Louella had told him once that old LPs are always difficult to sell. People suspect there must be something horrendously wrong with them -- which is generally not the case at all. They had simply been superseded by compact disks or cassettes. For a dime Hawley bought two records in a single jacket of the late poet Dylan Thomas -- one of his favorites -- reading from his own works, including his unfinished "Adventures in the Skin Trade."

After returning home, while comparing notes on the day's load of treasures, the Shorts listened with rapt attention to the sonorous voice of the Welsh poet, recorded before a live audience in New York City in 1952, a year before his untimely death. Mrs. Short produced cups of steaming hot chocolate shortly before the poet reached his marvelous description of an English tea room at a railroad station where "Cold stiff people with time to kill sat staring at their tea and the clock, inventing replies to questions that would not be asked, justifying their behavior in the past and future, drowning every moment as soon as it began to breathe, lying and wishing, missing all the trains in the terror of their minds, each one alone at the terminus. Time was dying all over the room."

"Wow!" Hawley interjected, jumping to his feet. Let's play that again!" And they did.

When they reached that same passage again -- "Time was dying all over the room" -- "Wow!" he exclaimed again.

"That's got it, how I feel about library sales and all the skillfully crafted old card catalogues that have already gone the way of the Phoenix. A bird whose life span, incidentally, was precisely half a millennium - the distance from Gutenberg to now when, to paraphrase the Welsh poet, 'time is dying all over the reading rooms of the world.'"

Chapter 14

GOOD OLD DAYS

Strangers in town, they had traveled a long way from Denver to reach Plymouth, Helen and McPhail -- or "Mac" as everybody called him -- O'Brien. The sky was so misty on the morning of their arrival that they could barely make out the letters carved in the weathered lintel over the entrance through their bifocals.

Yep, that's it!" Mac finally said, as Louella Winters hurriedly passed them on the sidewalk, sufficiently anxious to get inside before it rained that, uncharacteristically, she decided against trying to be helpful to this elderly pair of visitors.

"THE PLYMOUTH PUBLIC LIBRARY," Mac continued aloud. "And just about as old as we are if I'm reading those Roman numbers right. 1930."

"Speaks well for the community," Helen chimed in, straightening a skirt deeply wrinkled by several days journey in the car, and putting her gloves in her purse.

"Why, whatever do you mean by that, princess?" Mac asked.

"Well, that was the beginning of the Great Depression, dummy," she said. Like most women who have been married to the same man for nearly fifty years, she had a highly developed ability for putting him in his place. "Folks back then didn't have much money. But just look at the size of those granite blocks. Must have cost a pretty penny. Not to mention all the fancy millwork around the windows."

"Yep, you're right about that, Helen," Mac agreed, feeling somewhat encouraged by what she had said about his mother's generation.

By the time of their visit the O'Briens -- "Senior Citizens" -- had weathered the first and most difficult phase of the transition to retirement. Mac had gotten in a lot of fishing and golfing. At Helen's prodding, he had faithfully and dutifully finished painting the trim on their house and complied with a thousand and other requests she dreamed up to keep him busy.

She had about run out of ideas when late one evening, after watching a boring re-run of an old movie, Mac had said: "You know, Helen, I was thinking. I would kind of like to look up ma's folks back in Plymouth."

"But they're dead," said Helen, just to needle him, knowing full well what he had in mind.

"Oh, I know that," Mac persisted. "But I'd like to visit where they're buried, find out more about the sort of lives they led on the farm. Research the old family roots."

When Eric Motley saw the O'Briens enter the door, he knew at a glance why they had come. For he had assisted many couples at their particular stage of life. Moreover, with his own retirement looming up on the horizon, he was himself about ready to traverse the same terrain.

The only surprise for Motley was that the O'Briens, having arrived at his desk, first asked for the location of the restrooms. But once they had returned, his pride of profession was immediately restored. They asked him exactly what he knew they would ask.

He was ready with his response, suggesting that they begin in the Genealogy and Local History Room. "It's upstairs, first door to the right. You'll want to speak to my colleague, Mary Mountfort."

"And how may I help you?" Mary asked as she rose and came around her large, cluttered desk to shake their hands and find them a place for their soggy umbrella and coats.

"Well, we're the O'Briens from Denver," said Helen, after having waited in vain for Mac to take the initiative. But Mac was tongue-tied, apparently, determinedly staring off into space, his clear blue eyes vaguely aimed in the direction of the oil portraits ranged about the walls of Plymouth notables of the last century, all dressed in severe-looking black clothes.

Sensing the drift of his thoughts and seeking to assuage his natural timidity in the face of the past, Mary Mountfort brightly offered: "You know scholars say that the artists, who did portraits like these, pre-painted the clothes, while awaiting commissions to paint in the faces and hands."

"Izzat so?" Mac marveled in the stillness of a room where everybody's business soon becomes everybody else's business.

There was a soft, faintly audible tittering from two snow-white-haired volunteers, both freshly coifed by the same hairdresser, who were filing three by five cards on which had been typed information on births and deaths gleaned from local newspapers. They had heard the story before; it was always funny the way Mary told it.

Mary introduced the volunteers to the O'Briens. When one of them heard Mac saying that his given name was McPhail after his mother's maiden name -- "spelled M, small c, capital P, h, a, i, l," -- she looked up from her labor: "You know I knew a McPhail family once. They had a small farm a few miles out of town. If I'm not mistaken, they have a plot in the cemetery out near the Brighton road stop sign."

"Izzat so!" Mac exclaimed, dumbfounded by this sudden stroke of good luck -- this clue to what he had come so far to find out.

Before rushing off to follow up on this lead, Helen, as Mary Mountfort suggested, looked through a well-ordered collection of tattered old city directories. Wherever she found an entry for the McPhails, she inserted one of the slips provided by Mary.

Meanwhile, Mac, having rediscovered his tongue, was pumping the old volunteer, who had remembered something about the McPhail family, for anything she might remember about them or their plot in the cemetery. This gracious woman, while fielding his excited questions, took pains to make two carefully drawn maps, one showing the route to the Brighton stop sign, the other a schematic drawing of the layout of the cemetery.

Nearing completion of the latter under Mac's inquiring gaze, she said to him: "I think you will find the McPhail plot somewhere around the center of the cemetery, near the top of a rise in the terrain."

"Well, I'll be darned," Mac said, appreciatively. "I can't tell you how grateful we are for your trouble. Please, once more, what did you say your name was? We'll be wanting to send you a little something when we get back to Denver."

"There's no need to do anything of the sort," she said, "but if you insist, why here I'll give you a name. I'll just write it on the map."

Which she did in large block letters -- "MARY MOUNTFORT, THE PLYMOUTH PUBLIC LIBRARY."

Without looking at what she had written, Mac scooped up the paper, folded it carefully, and put it in his pocket. He could hear Helen softly calling him from across the room, and he didn't want to keep her waiting after she had come all this way to help him with his quest.

Helen had finished going through the city directories. She sent Mac downstairs to copy the pages where she had inserted slips before scanning the pages of other old books that Mary Mountfort had provided.

Downstairs, Mac, though a civil engineer by profession, soon discovered that the copier was a troublesome machine. Before he could operate it, shamefacedly he had to prevail upon Eric Motley to show him how it worked. Motley explained that first Mac had to feed some dollar bills into another machine, which issued a card that looked like a credit card. Then he had to insert this card into an appendage to the copying machine, where a mechanism lit up, indicating digitally how much money he had to his credit.

So far, so good. Mac was busily bending to the task of making copies when a funny-looking red light on the machine began flashing. At that precise moment Louella Winters poked her head out of her office. At once grasping what had gone wrong, she leaned over and opened up the copier, and adroitly cleared a paper jam.

"Think nothing of it," she said, as she watched to make sure it was functioning properly.

"Why, thank you so very much ma'am," said Mac, "and may I ask to whom I am indebted?"

"The librarian," Louella exclaimed, rushing toward her office to answer the phone.

"Didn't know that's what librarians did," said Mac affably.

"Neither did I," Louella responded before closing the door.

Having finished the library portion of their research, the O'Briens were so anxious to reach the cemetery that by mutual consent they decided to skip lunch, until fate suddenly intervened. For no sooner had they reached this decision than as Mac was driving up the main street, he felt a sudden, sharp pain in his chest and his upper torso being pulled forward, involuntarily, toward the steering wheel.

"Guess I'd better stop for one of those little pills," he said, pulling awkwardly into a convenience store near a gas station.

As this had happened before, Helen knew exactly what to do. She hurried inside for a cup of water. Mac, meanwhile, fumblingly retrieved a pill from a container in his jacket. By the time he had swallowed it along with the liquid, they could see that the obliging auburn-eyed Hispanic girl

109

with thick glasses who had provided the water was approaching to ask if there was anything she could do.

"No, I'll be all right," said Mac through the side window. "But sure do appreciate your thoughtfulness."

The young lady introduced herself as Maria Alvarez. As she turned to go, Helen couldn't resist the impulse to get out of the car and give her a hug.

"Say, I could use a cup of coffee," Helen said, "Mac, how about you? A hot chocolate and a sandwich might be just what you need. Maybe we shouldn't have skipped lunch after all."

"Oh, sure honey," Mac said, "and maybe Maria here would take a look at our map just to make sure we're on the right road."

Upon learning where they had been, Maria noted with pride that she was a member of the Council of the Friends of the library. She spoke very highly of Mary Mountfort, and confirmed that they had indeed started out right, even as she made them each a tasty sandwich.

Refreshed and reassured, the O'Briens continued their trip, Helen at the wheel, Mac at her side with the map spread out on his lap.

"Nice people hereabouts," he said.

Within about half an hour, they had reached the stop sign at Brighton road.

"Now take a right," Mac said, looking up from the map. "It should be on the left, on your side, in about a quarter of a mile."

"Glad we brought along our ponchos," said Helen, eyeing the glowering sky as they turned off into the cemetery and passed through an open gate, firmly anchored by large stone moorings. From their map it now appeared that they would have to proceed first through a modern section of the cemetery before reaching the older one they sought.

Driving slowly, Helen stopped from time to time to gaze at intriguing headstones. One had a laser etching of a young girl shooting a basket into a hoop up over what looked like a family garage. Another showed a young man standing proudly, polishing rag in hand, by the door of a shiny-looking convertible.

"Do ya 'spose that could be the car that killed him?" Mac asked aloud, reading an inscription that indicated the boy had died at the tender age of 19.

110

From there the well-graveled road became two winding dirt tracks, which led gradually up and around and into an older section of the cemetery, to judge from the look of the weathered stones. Helen slowed to a crawl to call Mac's attention to a shoulder-high sculpture of a tree. Its stone limbs were home to a pair of exquisitely carved squirrels and a deftly rendered nest of a family of robins.

"See how the tree is so unnaturally short in stature. That's the symbol for a life cut short," said Helen, "one of the many things I learned from Mary Mountfort while you were working the copier."

Finally, the dirt tracks ended abruptly at a sharp rise in the terrain. The shoulders of the trail were well beaten down, hardened under the weight of many cars that had parked there before them.

"Guess it's on foot from here on," Mac said as he retrieved their ponchos from the back seat. "No need to lock the car. There's no one going to bother it here."

Under darkening skies the quest for what they had come so far to find picked up in intensity. Feeling exhilarated, they quickened their pace.

"You take that side of the hill, and I'll take this," said Mac, suddenly feeling in charge and ordering his command. Helen willingly obeyed, for she had become a full and loving partner in this quest for his mother's grave, the physical evidence of the womb from whence he had sprung.

Moreover, she had fallen under that strange spell that only tombstones can cast, as she zigzagged back and forth on her side of the hill, drawn deeply into contemplation of those beneath her feet. People, as she imagined, who might have hated each other in life, lain side by side, to bicker for all eternity.

She was caught up, too, by a compelling curiosity to know more about the lives of some of those over whom she was passing, their histories briefly carved in stone. Loving wives, dear husbands, and sprinkled in and among them devoted children, some of whom had died in infancy, carried off by some malady that might easily be cured today. And everywhere the trite verses of poets past, too well remembered, and quotations from the Great Book -- the Bible.

How many glorious such field trips as Helen and Mac took that day have begun in some library? This is not to mention journeys among the living or to far-off places, adventures of the mind -- through books traversing remote realms, moor and mountain, even the farthest reaches of the universe and beyond. Nothing, not fantasy-inducing drugs, nor Saintly good works, nor the enjoyment of perfect health nor mountainous riches, provide the pleasures that an ordinary person can obtain at a local library free of charge.

The O'Briens were silently turning over their gratitude for that in their minds, as they stooped to their labor, reading the silent stones on a hillside where it was reward enough simply to be alive and able to read, where everything about them was dead, even the flowers, which had yielded their plumage in the late fall to the umbers without which no artist's palette is complete.

It took them three-quarters of an hour of thoughtful reverie to reach the crest of the rise, where they joined up to rest on a bench, thoughtfully provided for that purpose, and to gaze vacantly about. It was then that the errant sun, making an extraordinary effort, poked its head through the clouds briefly, casting a luminous ray of light on one particular stone.

"MCPHAIL!" they shouted in unison.

"That's it!" said Mac, "that's it! Oh, Holy be!"

And off he headed, Helen at his heels.

Though some of the letters were a bit faded, they could readily make out the inscription: "FLORENCE MCPHAIL O'BRIEN, 1895-1958." And beneath this: "HOME AT LAST."

"How beautiful," Helen sighed to Mac, who had removed his cap - something he didn't do all that often -- and nodded in agreement.

The sun lingered long enough for Helen to snap a couple of photos before she said: "Mac, I'm going on down to the car. You stay up here as long as you like. I have some knitting to do, so don't hurry."

Mac spent about half an hour by himself up there near the crest of the hill, oblivious to the patter of raindrops on his head, hat in hand.

When finally he came down, he planted a long kiss on Helen's lips. Though he was soaked through and through, she didn't complain.

Following a night spent at a motel outside of Plymouth, the O'Briens headed West. On the way home Mac was forever taking off his cap without being asked and doing little things for Helen that he had sort of neglected in recent years, opening and closing doors for her, making sure she got the first cup of coffee in the morning.

During their journey Helen described to Mac the fears that Mary Mountfort had confided as to the future of her department in the Plymouth library. How when she retired, Mary was positive that it, like the rest of the library, would be, as she had put it -- "com-pu-terror-ized."

Though he had never evinced much interest in libraries before, Mac listened intently and sympathetically. But his mind was mostly elsewhere, caught up with their discovery, the finding of his mother's plot in the cemetery, the things that Helen had read to him at the motel from the copies of the pages of old books.

"Can't wait to tell the guys!" he said on more than one occasion with the tone of voice of someone for whom the mysteries of the universe have suddenly been revealed.

"It's a good feeling," he explained to Helen, "before you die, to know where you came from. I have never felt so confident about who I am."

And on and on he rambled.

Nor was it boring to Helen, pleased that Mac's newfound interest in family lore had reawakened his increasingly quiescent faculties and sparked some of the old enthusiasm he had reserved for his job for so many years.

It was in January, in the depths of a bitter-cold winter, two months before she retired, that Mary Mountfort received a small package from Denver with a letter enclosed:

"I regret to say that Mac passed away shortly after Christmas," it began. "I can't remember a moment in our marriage that he was any happier than on our visit to Plymouth.

"Please inform that helpful volunteer who made the maps for us that we did indeed find the plot where his mother, Florence McPhail O'Brien, is buried, just where she had said it would be, near the crest of the hill. That meant so much to Mac. He said it made him feel fulfilled as he prepared to depart this life.

"Knowing the thoroughness with which you perform your job, that you would be writing to ask for it, I have enclosed a copy of Mac's death certificate and obituary for your records, and might I ask a favor -- that you place a bookplate in one of your books to mark his passing."

To this, Helen had added a postscript: "In about two weeks I am off for a journey of discovery myself, to research my own family roots in Ireland.

Hope the libraries there are as obliging as Plymouth's."

Upon opening the accompanying package, Mary discovered a box of chocolates, each individually wrapped in delicate gold foil. She gave the first one to Louella Winters, who had popped her head in the door, and asked: "Who are they from?"

On reading the note, Louella looked up to say: "Oh, mi-gosh. Why didn't you tell me? Didn't you know my mother's maiden name was McPhail? He must have been a cousin of mine."

All that remains to tell, to complete the story, is that Mary Mountfort's fears were soon to prove well-founded. No sooner would she retire than the Genealogy and Local History Room would yield its dear, familiar old ways to "progress." The cards there would be scattered across some landfill, as part of an inexorable process that no librarian across the land, not even one as strong-willed as Mary, can withstand.

Her successor would join the rest of the staff in staring at a computer screen, punching cold, lifeless keys, like some airline reservation clerk. Presiding over a sterile room, where holes were drilled through beautiful old tables to accommodate all the machines indispensable to storing and retrieving so-called "Information." A CD-ROM would replace the old city directories which, in due course, would be discarded. All of this would transpire under the sternly reproving gazes of the old Plymouth notables whose portraits hung on the walls, watching in horror as the records of their existence were obliterated to make way for the present, mindlessly.

Chapter 15

S TATE LOTTERY

As Larry Higgins reported, the unprecedented publicity about libraries had not fallen on deaf ears in Columbus, Ohio, where politicians eagerly jumped on board what cartoonists depicted as "The Library Bandwagon." For the state's legislators it was that rarest of issue, something they could all wholeheartedly support in bipartisan fashion without fear of reprisal at the ballot boxes.

And speak out about it they did, at prayer breakfasts and county fairs, and in sound bytes craftily geared to television, which they delivered whenever opportunity presented itself, even in response to questions which were about something else entirely, like joblessness and the collapse of the steel industry. With no wars to speak of and a modicum of prosperity reigning at least temporarily, books, reading, and the preparation of youngsters to participate in the Information Age enjoyed a rare moment in the Ohio media spotlight.

"I don't think we'll ever see anything else like it, at least not in our lifetime," said Hawley Short to his wife. "Why you know, our little library at this moment seems to be garnering more publicity than Cleveland's Rock and Roll Hall of Fame.

"And I am sure glad that Neal Barker introduced me to the wonders of E-mail. I've been deluging the nitwits who represent us down in Columbus with messages to do something in time for Ohio's bicentennial in the year 2003."

The clamor raised by Hawley and the friends of libraries all around the state achieved in amazingly short order its purpose, creating an unmistakable and undeniable public demand for some sort of action. Something to place a capstone on all the efforts to promote reading all around the nation, for which, of course, they, the politicians in Columbus, could immodestly take the credit.

In keeping with the spirit of the times, the lawmakers decided that this could only be some form of state lottery, with a pot big enough to attract the attention of every right-thinking Buckeye and safeguards sufficient to deny out-of-state people any share of the spoils. That much indeed had been already decided upon by an overwhelming political consensus by the date that hearings were convened in the largest and most sumptuously appointed chamber of the Ohio capitol.

The principal witness was none other than Plymouth's own Neal Barker, who was nattily attired and flanked by prestigious leaders of Ohio thought and culture, anxious to share his moment in the spotlight.

Neal set the stage skillfully.

"May it please the delegates," he said, "I would like to begin by noting the enormous contributions the state of Ohio, home of the Inventors Hall of Fame, has made to the technologically-feasible plan that I wish to lay out for realizing the twin objectives of increasing reading and computer-literacy. Thus enabling the rising generation of youngsters to participate fully in the future progress of our great nation.

"As part of my presentation there will be a hands-on demonstration of what I am describing, in which I will invite you to participate with the laptop computers at your places. Those who do so, incidentally, will become eligible to receive a little present from the town of Plymouth, whose cash value is well below the amount allowable by way of gifts to political officials like yourselves."

The joviality of his announcement elicited a round of laughter. One legislative aide quietly exited the chamber to find his boss, who had not yet shown up because he was lingering over coffee.

Having used a little humor to get their attention, Neal Barker noted that in preparation for this day he had studied the experience of the various types of lotteries conducted by the state of Ohio. These included the biweekly super lottery drawings with prizes beginning at $4 million and so-called "Kicker" prizes of $100,000, the Buckeye drawings five times a week with prizes of $100,000, the twice daily drawings of sequences of four and three numbers with prizes of $5,000 for a dollar investment in the former category, and prizes of lesser monetary value for various permutations of the numbers in all of the aforementioned games of chance, and finally, the myriad of ever-changing scratch-off tickets which allowed a buyer instantly to know whether he had won a prize and how much.

"As models," Neal continued, "I have also studied the various lotteries conducted by several other states and the multi-State lotteries in benefit of education, which are either in operation or in the works. As you know our governor has urged that we join in the multi-state lotteries, and thereby swell the size of the pot and the profits to our state. I have also benefited from the input and constant encouragement of the Council of the Friends of the Plymouth Public Library."

"He scarcely needed to credit us," said Hawley Short to his wife, as they watched the hearings live on a public television station. "What he is describing is all his idea, and I must say he has fulfilled his bargain with me magnificently. Moreover, I'm coming around to his way of thinking. Who is this honky to stand in the way of progress?

"Why don't we just listen to Neal?" said Mrs. Short, cutting off her husband indignantly.

"I'd also like to acknowledge the helpfulness of the college in Plymouth," Neal continued, "and college and university libraries around the state of Ohio, which have pioneered the way for what I am going to propose.

"It all began, in a manner of speaking, back on March 30, 1992, when a system called OhioLINK networked together the computerized catalogues of several academic libraries around our state. Through this system a scholar or student today at any one of some 70 such libraries in Ohio can search a composite catalogue with approximately twenty-five million books from a computer terminal in his own particular library.

"It's nothing short of amazing, and I am proud to say for the record that Ohio was the first state in the union with a system like this, which enables someone in a college library to obtain access to all these books by punching a couple of keys. Once he has done that, the system itself takes over. It asks whether he would like to search the composite catalogue by author, title or subject.

"Parenthetically, please allow me to explain that in the old days if a person wanted to consult a book in another college library he had two choices. He could either travel to the library or he could borrow it through a laborious process called 'inter-library loan,' by filling out a form which was forwarded by mail to the appropriate library. This process often absorbed weeks if not months.

"But not any longer. With the OhioLINK program he can request a book belonging to any of the 70 libraries belonging to the system simply by punching in the number assigned to his college, followed by his own identification number - a sequence of numbers that the system recognizes as belonging to that individual person and no one else.

"To complete the system all that's needed is a couple of vans driven by young people anxious to tour about the state. They deliver and return the books borrowed by the various institutions involved in the system. I should add that the cost of this service to the libraries is more than offset by the savings realized because with the OhioLINK system today a reality, they do not all need to buy certain expensive books for which the demand may be limited. If one library has these books the rest of the libraries don't need to acquire them, at least not within the state of Ohio."

Sensing that one or another of the legislators was dozing off, Neal regained his hold on their attention by saying: "Let's all try the system out. Come on now, it's time to log in."

Looking a bit perplexed the legislators looked at one another and at their aides seated behind them for the help, which Neal himself soon provided.

"Just depress the space bar on your laptops. Highlight OhioLINK and push Enter. Let's suppose that we all want to look up books by author. Highlight Author. Let's check out what Toni Morrison, an Ohio winner of the Nobel Prize for Literature, has written lately. Key the letters of her name, last name first, then a comma, then her first name, which is spelled T,O,N,I. Push Enter."

A hushed stillness enveloped the chamber as several legislators bent to their own first lesson in computer literacy.

As they fiddled with the keys, Neal appealed once again to their pride in an accomplishment that few, if indeed any, of them had ever heard about before his appearance that day. "For about 3,000 years previous to the breakthrough we achieved in Ohio in 1992 each sizeable library had to struggle to collect and pass on to future generations the accumulated record of human thought by organizing its collections independently. But that is no longer the case. By working together and using the new technology to everybody's advantage we have created at the college level here in Ohio a system that will enable us to take the next step that I am proposing.

"This is to network together all of the public libraries in our state. The Cleveland Public Library has already put in place a building block of this process, by developing a composite catalogue, like that of OhioLINK, within its 29 branches. This year the branch libraries within the Cleveland system will loan some 270,000 items to one another.

"If we first build a network of computerized public library catalogues in Ohio, rewarding Buckeyes for reading or achieving computer literacy by some form of state lottery would become relatively easy," he said, rising from his chair and standing in front of a visual display.

"You see, every time a patron at a public library checks out a book, his bar code -- which is like the pin number used to obtain access to bank accounts at automated teller machines -- is recorded. The more books checked out the more opportunities for the library patron to win whatever prize the Ohio legislature in its wisdom may dictate.

"What I am describing is not very advanced, nor even very novel. Credit card companies use essentially the same system I am suggesting to reward people who make purchases using their particular form of plastic card

"The bar-code revolution itself was touched off, I am proud to say, in Troy, Ohio on June 26, 1974. On that date a scanner, manufactured by the NCR Corporation of Ohio, whose headquarters is located in that vicinity, was passed over the bar code on a ten-pack of Wrigley's chewing gum at the Marsh Supermarket. The resultant price was registered in a cash register.

"Subsequently, of course, government agencies have made use extensive use of bar codes. Some states put them on drivers' licenses, and thereby help police to catch criminals. The bar code similarly helps libraries to apprehend people who negligently or malevolently are removing books without first checking them out.

"Now there are a lot of ramifications to even this simple system. Someone has suggested that we might consider rewarding authors in a somewhat similar manner. For example, every time someone publishes a book today, the book is given an International Standard Book Number, or ISBN. It would be entirely possible to enter that number, which is recorded at the national Copyright Office, in a separate drawing to reward writers.

"Someone else suggested that still another drawing might be held to reward the author whose books are checked out the most frequently. The possibilities to encourage creativity would seem to be limitless. Once we have the system in place - a state-wide composite computerized catalogue including all the libraries in Ohio -- publishing houses, printers and book distributors may well prove willing to finance some sort of system of rewards on their own in accord with their respective interests. This would not cost taxpayers a cent.

Neal paused for a few seconds to let this agreeable thought sink in before discussing the next subject.

"Now, turning to teaching computer literacy, I have a little demonstration for you. But first may I introduce Braxton Augustus. He's eleven years old. I will ask him to take a seat at the computer terminal tied into that screen over there against the wall.

"I will ask him to respond to certain questions which I have downloaded into the system. The first question, Braxton, is what two Presidents of the seven supplied by the state of Ohio were born in the same year?

"Before he answers I will allow you legislators to answer the question, to test your intelligence, so to speak."

There followed a brief interval filled with blank looks, consultations by those on the committee with their aides sitting behind them.

"As no one among you seems to have the answer, would you provide it, Braxton?"

With a broad grin Braxton keyed in and said aloud the correct answer. "It was Ulysses S. Grant and Rutherford B. Hayes, and the year was 1822."

At that point in the proceeding the chair of the committee, a woman, suggested that it was time for a short break so members might answer an important roll call vote on the floor.

Taking advantage of the opportunity, Neal invited members of the committee to try out the system he had worked out with Braxton's help. Braxton was surprised at how inept the representatives, who availed themselves of this opportunity, were in operating what seemed to his young mind a very simple computer program.

When the committee members were all back in their seats, Neal summarized very briefly what he had said up to that point.

"A system to reward people for reading is thus easily achievable within the context of our present technology. Moreover, by adding to bar codes

120

the dates of birth of library patrons, we could distribute those rewards by age, providing college scholarships, for example, to the best performers among seniors in high school.

"Now, I invite your attention to this bingo card distributed by the lottery of Ohio, which is like numerous such cards distributed by other states. To play it you have only to uncover the letters and numbers and see if you have achieved a bingo on any of the four cards. Any child playing such a game, were it offered on a computer, would be forced to become computer literate to find out if he has won a prize.

"What can be achieved through bingo could be achieved through similar computer-generated games featuring prizes for success in solving mathematics problems, answering questions in the fields of history or literature, for example. The only caveat I see, based on the experience of state lotteries already in operation, is that the prizes must be of sufficient size as to attract a good deal of media attention, or alternatively, so many prizes must be offered as to enhance the odds of maximum participation and winning.

"Finally and to reward your patience and participation, I am going to ask Braxton to present each of you with the little present I promised from the good people of Plymouth, Ohio."

"I wonder what that could be?" said Hawley Short, who had been glued to his television set, like most other people in Plymouth.

"Recycling buckets! Now if that doesn't beat all," said Mrs. Short.

Shortly before the television camera broke away from the scene at the animated hearing chamber in Columbus, they could see the legislator who had been tardy to the hearing raise two fingers as Braxton approached with his bucket.

"The rascal!" Hawley said to his wife. "On the other hand I suppose they have a lot to recycle down there in Columbus."

The following day the return of Neal and Braxton to Plymouth was cause for an immediate special meeting of the library's Friends Council.

"We have been having so many special meetings," said Lydia McGovern, "that perhaps it's time we just bowed to the inevitable and met regularly twice a month. And I hate to tell you this, Louella, but we're going to need a larger room to accommodate our numbers."

"Yes, I can see that," Louella replied, welcoming those who squeezed in around the table. Their numbers included Larry Higgins, Brian Hedley, the head of the leather-jackets -- whose mechanized associates had just been hired as escorts and couriers for the Hollywood production company which would soon be arriving to shoot the pilot episode of "The Friends of the Library" -- and Braxton Augustus, who found a box to sit on at Neal Barker's side.

"I think we can all be proud of Braxton," said Neal, who opened the discussion by reporting on the very positive reaction to their joint appearance in Columbus, "and the way he demonstrated the computer literacy idea to legislators and their aides."

"Yes, and I'm here to tell you that not one of them was half as well informed as the people who work here in this library," Braxton chimed in, smiling broadly.

"So what's the next step in developing the lottery idea?" asked Preston Myers impatiently.

"The way I understand it," said Neal, "is that the governor will shortly appoint an advisory commission to work out a proposal more or less along the lines I suggested. In due course the commission will submit to the legislature the specifications for a piece of legislation, tentatively entitled 'The Ohio Reading and Computer Literacy Lottery Bill.' "

"What kind of bottom line are we talking about?" asked Preston, the light of greed shining in his eyes.

"Well if you mean money-wise," Neal replied, "the figure I heard is on the order of $25 million."

"Wow!" said the leatherjacket, turning to Braxton, "do you 'spose you could teach me how to run one of those machines?"

His remark elicited laughter around the table, as people refilled their mugs with bitter-tasting coffee.

Meantime, the hearings in Columbus had already generated a landslide of publicity on the lottery proposal and the airing in the media of a startling array of ingenious and creative ideas, which provided fodder for animated discussion around the table.

"I see here," said Charles Whitney, passing around a newspaper clipping, "that some professor at the local college has suggested that we might use a state lottery to cut into voter apathy. His idea is that Ohio could offer randomly awarded prizes to attract voters, the size of the prizes larger in years when the political choices facing voters seem particularly dull or uninspired."

"That would be every year," interjected Hawley Short, "and why not? You remind me that I must call that young reporter from <u>The Plain Dealer</u>, and urge again that his newspaper run an editorial suggesting the substitution of a pair of dice for the bald eagle as our national symbol."

"Oh, come on, Hawley," said María Álvarez. "This is happy news that Neal has provided. Don't spoil it."

"You're right," said Hawley. "You're right, and I apologize for sounding a sour note on this day, of all days, when Neal and Braxton have provided so much to cheer about."

"Hear! Hear!" interjected Larry Higgins, giving María's hand a little squeeze under the table.

"And now, how about Hollywood?" asked Louella Winters, turning to Brian Hedley.

"Well, get ready!" said Brian, grinning from ear to ear. "My script has been approved, which doesn't mean they won't turn it upside down and inside out once they're on location here in Plymouth. The financial end of it is all in place thanks in part to all the sponsors, who are hoping to cash in on Neal's lottery idea. What's next? That would be the arrival here in Plymouth of Mr. Vance LePage himself and his entourage escorted by a fleet of Harley Davidsons."

Chapter 16

HOLLYWOOD

The news that a television production crew from Los Angeles was coming to film a pilot episode of "The Friends of the Library" was headlined on the front page of the Gazette in large block letters from the font reserved for major events, like power outages, championship soccer teams, or local drug busts. "Every man, woman and child in Plymouth seems ecstatic about our town's impending celebrity," the newspaper said in an accompanying editorial, "the moment when our community, a typical flatlands settlement in northeast Ohio, will be transformed by the magic of Hollywood into something worth seeing."

There was a flurry of activity all over town, as people in Plymouth got ready for this cosmic change. Homeowners repainted houses that didn't need repainting, put new roofs on homes that wouldn't need them in the normal course of events for several years. The members of Plymouth's garden club were out in full force from dawn until dark, replanting beds of flowers, which had been perfectly okay and weed-free the day before. The local tree trimming service experienced a boom in business, responding to stacked-up calls on its answering machine to remove unsightly dead branches.

Nor were local commercial establishments oblivious to the prospects raised by the arrival of Hollywood. Broken sidewalks were repaired all over downtown Plymouth. The coffee shop installed a gas-powered lamp that gave off an old-time glow. Both the bank and hardware store installed smart and expensive new signs, advertising their services with raised gold letters on handsome black backgrounds. The Chamber of Commerce hired a local artist to freshen up the signs on approaches to the town from all four directions.

"What better time than now!" became the operable phrase in Plymouth.

With Hollywood on the way, the town's recreation department installed the new playground equipment it had promised for years in parks frequented by children. The Fire Department acquired the expensive and shiny new engine for which it had long hankered. A local church made use of the engine's cherry-picker to replace the slightly tilted cross above its belfry with one made of impermeable aluminum that sparkled in the sunlight. As a precaution the town's emergency response team was on hand with a brand new vehicle, equipped with the latest in life-saving gear.

What was true of Plymouth's infrastructure extended to the residents of the town. Tailoring establishments reported record sales of sports jackets and designer jeans. Hair-trimming salons likewise did a thriving business. Women who used to get a hair cut or permanent once-a-month, did so now on a semi-monthly or even weekly schedule. The owner of a laundry was amazed when people, who had been washing their shirts at home for years, brought them in to be professionally done with plenty of starch and on hangers.

Nor was the excitement over the prospective arrival of a television crew limited just to Plymouth. For word of the coming of Hollywood soon spread like a prairie wildfire in the surrounding area. With the result that the population of Plymouth, four thousand, seemed to double. To accommodate as many patrons as possible, the proprietors of eating establishments set out tables on the crowded sidewalks. There were long lines every evening at the town's movie theater, whose owner had replaced all the dead light bulbs on the marquee for the first time in anyone's memory. The sale of popcorn inside was extraordinarily brisk, even on nights when the weather was inclement and the featured attraction something less than spectacular.

"Would you believe it?" Hawley Short commented to María Álvarez one morning while picking up a newspaper and resisting his longing for a donut, "the way this town has gone nuts, and all because of a few reels of celluloid."

"Oh, I don't know," said María, smiling the smile that says a woman wants to tell somebody something. "I like to think that all the painting and scrubbing up has a more lofty purpose, like getting ready for a wedding."

"Why whatever put that into your head, dear girl, or do you know something I don't?"

"At the moment the answer is 'yes,'" said María, pushing up her glasses on her nose to reveal eyes radiant with happiness.

"Then tell me!" said Hawley, impatiently.

"Oh, no, I would much rather just show you," said María, extending the fingers of her left hand, slightly coiled to show to maximum advantage a sparkling diamond ring.

"Then it's Larry and you," said Hawley. "How wonderful! How wonderful! And there is a reason indeed for the people of Plymouth to get excited. Thank you for telling me, and as this is a special occasion, let's both have a donut."

Hawley could scarcely wait to reach home to tell his missus.

But before he left, he embraced María and said, "Larry is a lucky man. You know a wife is wonderful thing to have and, conversely, a husband is a wonderful thing to have, as you may learn for yourself in due course, about the time you reach my age."

"Thank you for that beautiful thought," said María, blushing deeply.

Later on that morning in late summer the members of the advance team from Hollywood arrived in Plymouth. Their sun-bronzed faces stood out among the pale visages of locals. This made it easy to chart the comings and goings of the newcomers, which became the main topic of conversation everywhere. Their most casual remarks were widely and often inaccurately quoted, on the streets and in the eateries, at churches or places of work.

"Will there be a demand for local people to perform as extras in the filming?" someone asked a member of the advance team in the rest room at the coffee shop.

His reply, "I dunno, I'm just an advance man," was quickly translated by the gossip circuit into "You know, I hear they might use a lot of local people. The best spot to be, of course, is over at the library."

The remark soon reverberated around town, and prompted people to wonder if it just might be a good time to put a few dollars in some books or insert a bookplate in some new work the library had acquired, to honor a forgotten friend they had suddenly remembered. Nor were the members of the library staff themselves immune to the possibilities, as they furtively looked up from their computer screens to watch the advance crew plotting out the places to film scenes, or measuring distances and making blue chalk marks on the floor by special permission of the Friends Council.

Even Louella Winters found herself dressing a little more smartly, just in case she might, inadvertently, pass before the lens of a camera. The dour Dwight Moodey took to wearing a necktie on the job -- something he had only rarely done before. The two young ladies behind the circulation desk showed up daily with fresh flowers in their hair, their mouths thick with lipstick. The venerable Eric Motley went so far as to buy a new jacket, which, before sitting down behind the reference desk, he hung on the back of his chair as he had the old one.

Amid many such subtle and not-so-subtle reminders that celebrity was about to pass their way, the people of Plymouth anxiously awaited what the Gazette called "their rendezvous with destiny." In keeping with the spirit of that cliché, the anticipation of men, women, and children of the town was positively at fever pitch, when finally a convoy of rental vans, escorted by a fleet of Harley Davidsons, arrived at the library. On board were members of the cast, a half dozen screenwriters -- including Brian Hedley -- cameramen, film editors, prop people, set designers, gaffers, and all the various other categories of professionals, which figure in a Hollywood production.

Director-producer Vance LePage rode in lordly splendor at the head of the procession. Preston Myers practically swooned in welcoming him on behalf of the Friends of the Library. Plymouth's mayor was similarly effusive in his words of greeting to LePage and muscled his way in next to the great man for a photo by one of his aides, for use in his campaign brochure in the next election.

Meanwhile, the Gazette's only reporter strained to take down verbatim their words on what the newspaper would characterize as "an occasion that would live in Plymouth history." The paper's editor sought to catch everything on his new tape recorder, just in case the reporter missed something. Two newspaper photographers, one more than the number carried regularly on the newspaper's payroll, ranged far and wide, snapping pictures of the members of the cast, the production crew, and excited faces in the crowd, for the Gazette's planned special 12-page commemorative issue.

From thenceforth the presence of the celebrities from Hollywood dominated all civil discourse in Plymouth. Their activities, hour by hour, and minute by minute, were a matter for intense scrutiny. The style of caps they wore set instant fashion trends. What they had for breakfast, lunch and dinner became subjects of compelling interest. They were discussed and re-discussed wherever people ran into one another on the streets, in church, or on the golf course.

And when the filming was in progress, a large percentage of Plymouth's population congregated in and around the library. Blue-collar workers found reason to convey their lunch buckets to the greensward in front of the building instead of somewhere along the creek, which heretofore had been their preferred place to picnic. In the process they transformed the park-like area into a human rookery, to the irritation of those who had to mow the grass.

Meanwhile, inside the library the press of rubber-neckers was so thick that on one occasion that the production crew had to call a halt to its operations. In frustration Vance LePage threw up his hands and shouted "If you don't stop milling about, all you people, we're going to have to find another library to shoot our story."

His exhortation had the desired effect of thinning the hordes for the rest of that day. On another, when oglers were back again in full force, Brian Hedley quietly whispered something into LePage's ear, which drew a chuckle and quick action. LePage dispatched a gaffer and a camera with no film at all in its chamber out onto the lawn with instructions to feign filming a mob scene requiring a multitude of extras. The ruse worked well enough that LePage employed it quite often on subsequent days.

But when people in Plymouth got wind that it was to be the final day of filming, LePage had to summon Louella Winters to the rescue. To clear out the library for a sequence of quiet scenes, she pulled the fire alarm, which produced an ear-splitting sound. While she made pretense that this might be the real thing, people streamed out of the building, and Plymouth's fire chief, whom she had tipped to her ploy, appeared at the scene dressed in a bright yellow slicker, aboard the Department's new engine. His men, as instructed, feigned frantic action -- uncoiling their hoses and hooking them up to hydrants and stretching a yellow tape beyond which people from thenceforth were not allowed until the filming was finished.

Of such were the high-jinks and amusements during the shooting that after three weeks, when the film-makers packed up all their equipment, the strobe lights and cameras and over-sized film cans, and departed under motorcycle escort, it was a sad day in Plymouth. In a letter to the editor of the <u>Gazette</u> someone suggested flying the pennant-shaped Ohio flag over city hall at half-mast. The paper was inundated with letters of advice from various and sundry people, with suggestions on how to cope with post-Hollywood-production depression.

"Let's face it, we knew it couldn't last," a psychologist wrote, advising people to take up a new hobby, or try a new, widely advertised pill to cope with sudden mood swings. He also cautioned that it would be a long time before people in Plymouth would know if all their effort had borne fruit, or merely been in vain.

He was right about that. It proved to be a long wait indeed, during the seemingly interminable months of northern Ohio winter, which seem to last forever, while off in Los Angeles a film editor performed his magic, cut and spliced scenes, made them mesh with the voiced-over dialogue and musical interludes. Meanwhile, people in Plymouth hoped against hope that the takes in which they might have appeared, passing by a camera on the streets or in the library reading room, might end up, against all reasonable prospect, in the finished reel for the show rather than on the cutting room floor.

Finally, the day, or more precisely the evening, when such questions arising from human vanity would be definitely answered, arrived. At precisely five minutes before eight p.m., Hawley Short removed the dust cover from a little-used television set.

"We don't want to be late for this," he said, as his wife settled into a comfortable chair.

They were both prepared for the worst.

"I don't know that I'm up to watching this," said Hawley, ruminating on all the perfectly good books that had been made into terrible movies. Mrs. Short nodded in agreement, while softly stroking the cat that burrowed contentedly into her lap.

"At least it's what they call a pilot episode," Hawley continued, "which means that once it's over, it's over! There will be no more like it, barring a miracle."

"We can always hope that's the case," said Mrs. Short, as Hawley turned down the sound during an advertisement for automobiles.

He turned it up again in time to see the credits roll and hear the sound of a slightly wistful solo played on an oboe.

"That's a nice touch," Hawley said, as the camera panned up the exterior of the tall set of doors and came to rest on the stone lintel in which was chiseled PLYMOUTH PUBLIC LIBRARY.

"Oh mi-gosh!" exclaimed his wife, when the title of the projected series flashed on the screen -- "FRIENDS OF THE LIBRARY" and underneath a credit line, saying "based on an interactive novel by Hawley Short."

"That's decent of him, the producer Vance LePage, I mean," said Hawley. "He said he would grant me one wish in connection with the pilot, and I told him that it would please me mightily if he could make some reference to 'interactive,' for that was my whole idea in putting the ten dollars in those books, and everything that has transpired since -- to stir up people to act, to do something in the spirit of a friend of a local library."

While they both watched with keen anticipation, the camera moved slowly back to reveal the sturdily built, weathered structure from an artist's perspective.

"Doesn't our old library look grand?" Hawley said, letting out a little squeal of delight as the camera backed slowly away from the building constructed of large blocks of sandstone, several of them pock-marked by hastily-made intrusions to accommodate all the cables and conduits which constitute a modern library's life-support system.

Still she was a proud old dowager, Hawley thought, as the plaintive oboe trailed off, and gave way to the sound of gentle drums.

The camera moved briefly farther away to reveal the environs of the once genteel middle-class neighborhood, as the sound of the drums reached an ear-splitting crescendo, before going to a close-up of the copying machine whose red light was flashing "PAPER JAM! PAPER JAM! PAPER JAM!"

A slightly built young African-American woman dealt the machine a smashing blow with the heavy shoe on her clubfoot.

"Wow!" said a handsome young man of about her age, who was standing off to the side. "You pack quite a wallop!"

"It's my secret weapon," she said of the deformed extremity on which he had his eyes fixed. "You need all of them you can find, when you're a librarian."

The machine, meantime, returned to normal, and the red light stopped flashing.

"Then you're just the person I want to see," he said, smiling, "the librarian."

Chapter 17

WEDDING BELLS

In the weeks that followed the airing of the pilot episode, the pages of The <u>Plymouth Gazette</u> looked more like those of <u>Variety</u> than of a small weekly in northeast Ohio. The office of the newspaper, similarly, took on an odd appearance, as the handful of staffers spent hours with their eyes glued to a television set, to catch the latest show-business buzz about how the American public had reacted to the novelty of an hour-long show in prime time that could be safely viewed by everyone, even children.

Finally, after what seemed an interminable wait, the <u>Gazette</u> carried the news that everyone in Plymouth was anxiously awaiting, a banner headline proclaiming: "FRIENDS OF THE LIBRARY TO BE NETWORK SERIES." The story, which occupied the entire front page, was accompanied by a flurry of reports inside the newspaper, playing up the town's reaction to this development of cosmic importance.

"It will sure put us on the map!" enthused a local schoolteacher under a broadly smiling photo of herself.

"Our town is really very photogenic," said the proprietor of a small local nursery, who was pictured in the pilot, planting some azaleas in front of a church.

As people in Plymouth are seldom bashful when it comes to telling other people how to go about their business -- particularly outsiders -- the letters to the editor page was awash in thoughts about how Hollywood should proceed in developing the series. There were numerous suggestions, for example, on Hollywood stars who might do a better job that those featured in the pilot episode. One letter writer suggested that a maximum of local people should be employed in future episodes as extras, or to make cameo appearances, "to lend the series authenticity."

There was substantial controversy over the portrayal of the librarian as a woman with a clubfoot. Several letter-writers found this objectionable. Among them was a lawyer who suggested that Louella Winters might even have grounds to file a suit for defamation and that he would be willing to file it pro bono -- for nothing. Somebody else suggested an upbeat resolution of the matter, how in a subsequent episode the person playing Louella's role might have her physical defect corrected by an operation at the Cleveland Clinic, paid for by grateful library patrons.

In a special box on the editorial page it was recorded that the Town Council had commissioned a local artist to paint signs, which were to be posted prominently on all roads leading into the town, saying: "PLYMOUTH, OHIO -- HOME TOWN OF 'THE FRIENDS OF THE LIBRARY' TELEVISION SERIES." These words, according to the mayor, who claimed credit for the idea, would be superimposed on a sketch of the library.

"I am reminded of Sauk Centre, Minnesota," Hawley Short said, showing the box to his wife. "You will remember, my dear, how on approaching that fair village in Minnesota, we saw those huge billboards proclaiming 'HOME TOWN OF SINCLAIR LEWIS.' One might have thought local people would have wanted to forget all about how they had been satirized in Main Street, as religious bigots and hypocrites.

"Ah, but here's happier news," Hawley continued, "about the impending marriage of our very own María Álvarez and Larry Higgins, who has been embraced, and rightly so in my opinion, as something of a local hero, since going public with his true identity, as undercover detective in the employ of New York publishing houses.

"I see the public is invited to the affair which, thanks to the special approval of our mayor -- he does seem to be sticking his nose into everything, doesn't he? -- and the Plymouth City Council, is to take place at the library itself. This will be a first in Plymouth history, the story notes. The cost of the affair is to be defrayed by 'generous, anonymous donors,' Hawley continued, who as I can tell you for your private information include Charles Stringfellow and Preston Myers -- the latter dying to tell people just how generous he is being, but sworn to secrecy."

The day of the wedding in May proved gloriously beautiful. The grounds of the old Plymouth library were resplendent, thanks to the uncompensated toil of the father and son team of Gerald and Braxton Augustus. Gerald had been assisting Eric Motley at the reference desk since being released from prison, and devoted every available hour of his free time to cultivating the plants in beds along the sidewalks. Braxton worked under Gerald's watchful eye, happy at last to be reunited with the father who held the ladder for him as he scurried up and cleaned the windows inside and out.

For a touch of color, "THE FRIENDS OF THE PLYMOUTH LIBRARY" banner, which Lydia McGovern had made by sewing gold letters on a red background, flew over the main entrance. The further addition of patriotic bunting, draped beneath the windows outside, gave the venerable old structure a certain fin-de-siècle elegance, Hawley Short thought.

"An entirely apt reminder," he said to his wife as they joined the happy throng of people assembled for the nuptials, "of the time when great libraries of ornate style and architectural splendor were being built in the capital cities of the Western world -- Paris, Rio de Janeiro, our own Washington D.C.

"Before that all really ornate buildings, cathedrals excepted, were devoted to the pleasures of kings or tyrants, for the exclusive enjoyment of some monarch and his family. I have never understood why people are so curious about seeing them, and go to great expense and travel great distances to see what's in 'em, gilded chamber pots and ballrooms.

"Whereas they might instead devote their energies into visiting some of the world's great libraries, places which serve some purpose, and in whose construction no expense was spared. Structures designed not for royal courts or imperial governments, but where people might exercise and expand their brains by reading books. Library buildings that constitute a real triumph for democracy, which speak more eloquently and certainly more rationally of faith in the future than castles, or even churches or grand cathedrals, for that matter. Of course, that's just my opinion."

As the Shorts walked slowly toward the library, Hawley droned on and on about how the United States of America of today is the home of more than 150 libraries housing more than one million books each. This was not to mention, as he did, the more than 15,000 public libraries serving communities like Plymouth.

The vibrant sound of Mariachis, their violins and guitars sending up the warm, hot-blooded tunes of old Mexico and the revolution, drowned out his words, but still he persisted: "María told me once that she had promised

134

her grandfather, before he died, to have Mariachis at her wedding," Hawley said, though it was doubtful that his wife heard him.

She had fled beyond his reach, to the Ladies Room to adjust her hat and veil, leaving him, perfunctorily, to greet Mrs. Preston Myers. Her interests in life extended no further than the local golf course, where she was a regular patron sunshine or rain. The latter sort of days allowed her ample opportunity to indulge herself at the club's bar, where she always ordered, after carefully reviewing the entire list of available potions -- "her only reading" -- as Hawley once observed to his wife -- a brandy and soda.

While Hawley was rummaging in his brain for a topic that might prove of interest to Mrs. Myers, her husband joined them, wearing an enormous carnation in his lapel.

"Say, Preston, I have learned through various and sundry back channels of your generosity on this occasion, and I congratulate you for it. Might I just add that there is no one I admire more in the whole history of these United States than Andrew Carnegie."

"Why him of all people?" inquired Myers, who was enormously pleased that at least Hawley was privy to his generosity.

"Well, you must certainly know, or if you don't, allow me to tell you, that it was old Andrew Carnegie himself who single-handedly contributed the money -- and often the plans, as well -- for thousands of public libraries, including this one. Most of them are still standing, and still in busy use, though, of course, owing to technology they have been transformed into institutions which are a far cry from what he originally envisioned -- places that were simple to use, where people could improve upon themselves and get ahead."

"Sounds eminently sensible to me," said Myers, stifling a yawn.

Encouraged, Hawley forged on, "If I may enlighten you on a matter dear to my heart, you will recall that in the old days patrons almost invariably found the same arrangements in Carnegie libraries. On entering you ran smack dab into the card catalogue, the altar of knowledge. Off to the right was the reference room; off to the left Business, and upstairs Literature on the right and History on the left -- everything you needed.

"Simplicity of operation and accessibility were the hallmarks of the Carnegie library. While there were children's books, there were no children's rooms, no copying machine rooms, no community rooms, no

135

record and compact disk rooms, no video rooms, no senior citizens rooms, no computerized catalogue room, no rooms set aside for the display of art or to collect blood. The only machines in the era of which I speak were telephones and typewriters, whose presence was masked by thick interior walls.

"The patrons themselves on any given day could range around large tables on sturdy chairs sufficient to their purpose, but not so comfortable as to be conducive to napping. Moreover, the only posted sign -- again by contrast with today -- was perhaps a free standing reminder on top of the card catalogue, reminding patrons that they could look up books by author, title, or subject. And there were a lot of people, myself included, who thought that this was unnecessary -- an insult to people's intelligence."

While Hawley droned on and on, in Louella Winters' office, which had been converted into a dressing room for the occasion, Eric Motley, who was a lay minister, carefully adjusted his cassock and clerical robes with the help of Gerald Augustus.

"I must tell you," said Gerald, beholding Eric in full ministerial splendor, "that you make one mighty fine looking preacher."

"Why thank you, Gerald," said Motley. "Which reminds me I wonder if anyone has reminded Larry Higgins of that old saw to the effect that a man never knows how truly unimportant he is until his wedding day."

As it was a beautiful day, the wedding was celebrated outside, near the beds of peonies, which were in full bloom. It was thus that María Álvarez and Larry Higgins were joined in holy matrimony. Young Braxton Augustus, turned out in a flashy sports coat and sparkling black shoes, served as ring bearer.

The reception that immediately followed the service was held in the main reading room which had been transformed for the occasion under the joyous direction of Dwight Moodey by the same leather-jacketed youths who had been so helpful in collecting books for the sale. All of the machines and computer screens were unplugged for the day, and hidden from view by the cardboard boxes in which they had arrived, which were covered by table cloths set with vases of flowers, and little trays and bowls of nuts and delicacies.

The circulation desk was bedecked with fine linens on which reposed bottles of champagne in ice-filled silver buckets. The wedding cake, an artistic baker's rendering of the Plymouth library, rested on the linen-covered copying machine down the hall toward Louella's office.

Nor was a single mechanical device, including the copier, plugged in that day, even after the bridal couple had departed down the main stone steps amid a hail of rice and confetti.

Louella was the last to leave. On Charles Stringfellow's arm, she paused briefly before locking the door to revel in the stillness.

"You can all just hang out and take it easy," she said aloud, with a gesture toward all the mechanical gadgets, "until tomorrow, when the battle of the Plymouth Public Library begins anew."

"Maybe, you could just leave it all as it is for a while," said Charles, as they descended the steps, "in case somebody else would like to get married, which reminds me there is something I have been meaning to ask you."

"Not now!" said Louella, who was feeling a bit giddy, though she was very curious to know what he had in mind.

Chapter 18

M RS. ROOSEVELT

"Greater love hath no man or woman than to read the book of another," Hawley was writing on a copy of his novel that he intended to give to an acquaintance, when Mrs. Short put in her first appearance on a beautiful summer morning.

"What is so rare as a day in June, to quote the poet," he said, looking up at her, his face illuminated by the sunshine streaming through the windows. "And may it please a recording angel to note that the year of 2000, the last of this century and millennium, is proceeding very nicely indeed at least here in Plymouth. And look-ee here! my dear, through the glass of the front door. What a stroke of genius that was on your part -- your suggestion that we plant zinnias in the pots on our top step! They are ramrod erect and smartly turned out in my favorite colors from an artist's palette."

"Right on time for your birthday, too" said Mrs. Short."

"Ah, yes, I'd not forgotten that little detail," said Hawley, "amid my natural excitement over all of the glorious events, which have cast our community and our beloved library in the spotlight.

"Before retiring I was reading this separately-bound, little talk that first lady Eleanor Roosevelt gave at the Carnegie library in Washington, D.C., when the nation was mired in the Great Depression. It has the title 'What Libraries Mean to the Nation.' At that time, she lamented that many of the nation's states were spending only a dime or less per capita annually for library books. There were other states covering vast geographical areas, she said, where there were few books and even fewer libraries.

"She urged her listeners to do something about it. Here's what she said, and I quote her words: 'We have got to make our libraries the center of a new life in the mind, because people are hungry to use their minds,' she declared. 'We are facing a great change in civilization, and the

138

responsibility, I think, for what we do with our leisure time is a very great responsibility for all of us who have intellectual interests.'

"Of course, in her day, as she noted, the rise in the popularity of radio and the movies was threatening the survival of reading, though she believed that if these new media were properly channeled they could even reinforce and stimulate reading.

"How appropriate that is to our day! You have only to substitute television and the internet for radio and movies," said Hawley, "and we're back to what Mrs. Roosevelt was talking about. And, as in her day, we have got to do something about it. Use the latest wave of entertainment gadgets, which so distract people during their leisure time from developing their intellects.

"I'm beginning to think that we have arrived at a crossroads similar to the one Mrs. Roosevelt described. I no longer have those nightmares I used to have about machines. Neal Barker is right even if he sometimes uses the wrong reasons. The computer is not here to bridge a racial divide that originated in the library, as he sometimes implies, though I don't think he really means it, but as a possible means of humanity's salvation. I think that Neal is absolutely right about that.

"What's encouraging to me and to him, too, I think, is that in keeping with the old Biblical injunction that 'the meek shall inherit the earth,' the librarians, whose collective hallmark is humility, have at least the temporary custody of this infinitely powerful instrument. That may change because I think what Dwight Moodey says is also partly right. The library that we grew up loving is headed for oblivion. It may one day be possible to put everything that a library used to represent -- except its ambience -- in a single computer chip. Such patrons as still enjoy reading may simply print out the books they wish to borrow on their home computers. Sort of frightening, isn't it?"

"It's quite a philosopher I seem to have married,' said Mrs. Short.

"No, not much of a philosopher, but a happy, if somewhat confused, man," he said, giving her a little peck on the cheek.

"Think of what we've all accomplished in the past two years. People all over our great country are putting money in books to stimulate reading, though they are not being as generous as they used to be. Moreover, the American people have been awakened to all of the demands they are making of libraries without sufficiently funding them.

"Thanks to Lydia McGovern, the dearly deceased are remembered everywhere in a terribly meaningful way, I think, with bookplates in places where knowledge is still alive.

"Youngsters like Braxton Augustus -- and I have become so fond of him and of his father, too -- are everywhere becoming computer literate. How I hate that term. It demeans literacy, makes it sound as if computer literacy itself were a substitute for reading, which it is not. I wish someone would find another way of saying it, to make it convey the meaning that computer literacy is an 'accompaniment' of reading, in line with what Mrs. Roosevelt said of radio and the movies.

"That said, I see a real future for computers in the children's rooms. Down with Power Rangers and up with instruction in how to operate machines that have become -- let's face it -- indispensable in this day and age.

"Moreover, our own computerized catalogue seems to be operating now almost all the time without a hitch. Louella Winters said to me just recently that she's beginning to experience whole days without computer anxiety, has quit taking those prescription pills, entirely. The computer, of course, is no substitute to my way of thinking for the old card catalogue, and isn't it wonderful that our catalogue is enjoying a second life, if only in a prison? We must get down there some day, and experience the old pleasure of letting our fingers play along the tops of the cards.

"By the way our book thief, Charles Stringfellow, if you ask me, and you didn't, is very sweet on Louella Winters. Now that he is out of jail, I understand he is taking an unpaid position as coordinator of the nation's prison libraries.

"Stringfellow sort of rubbed it in, when he told me about it, saying that the future of reading, not to mention the futures of prison inmates, may depend in part on the selection of the right books -- books with a high moral, as well as intellectual content. That was of interest to Dwight Moodey, who volunteered to help Stringfellow in their selection.

"About the only fly in the ointment is that the libraries, our own included, keep on selling books out of their collections when they should hang on to them. But we may even be able to find a way around that disheartening problem with the royalties we will be receiving from the weekly 'Friends of the Library' series on television, thanks to the deal Charles Whitney worked out with the Hollywood rascals.

"According to him, we may well earn enough money from our royalties into the indefinite future to build a massive storage place for all of the cast-off books that all of the true friends of libraries, like us, are acquiring everywhere in the land.

"Wouldn't that be something?

"A place that a couple like us might like to retire, spend the golden years after our golden years, so to speak.

"Moreover, I understand that on election day the Ohio state lotteries, along the lines Neal Barker suggested, will be awarding millions of dollars to readers of books and the newly computer-literate. Am I right? Has this become a gamble-ocracy or not?

"And to cap it all off, though no cap is needed, did you hear that the likely next first lady of the land was once a librarian, and has organized the books in her home according to the Dewey Decimal system. On the down side her husband, our likely next President -- his definition of a bibliographer is 'the person who wrote the Bible' -- doesn't read books at all. But it would still be a highly desirable first, to have a librarian first lady," said Hawley, little foreseeing that this possibility would be worked out in the Tallahassee County Public Library, where the key votes of a disputed Presidential election would be counted and recounted.

Bubbling over with the good news, Hawley Short swung his green book bag over his shoulder, bound for the place where the sum total of human knowledge is available daily free of charge.

At the library, he found Dwight Moodey in a characteristically dour mood. "It is only the stubborn nature of the species librarianus that prevents it from seeing, like the dodo bird, the evident signs of its soon-to-be extinction," he said to Hawley, reading from something he was writing on his typewriter - the last one in the library.

"So clearly laid out is the road to the librarian's oblivion that it is only the dim-witted who can fail to see the signposts," Moodey droned on. "And how will future generations remember today's librarian? Those with a certain nostalgia for the past will think warmly of him."

"Stop!" said Hawley Short, raising both of his hands. "Much as I like you, Dwight, I am in no mood for depressing thoughts this day, though I will concede that of all those, who toil in libraries, you and your counterparts -- those in charge of acquisitions -- have suffered the most from the invention of the computer.

Before departing the library Hawley pressed on his dear friend a much-enlarged copy of a passage from a book called <u>A Place on the Glacial Till</u> by a biology professor named Thomas Fairchild Sherman. In his retirement Sherman had drawn on the notebooks, which recorded numerous field trips with his students, to describe the area where Plymouth is located. In poetic fashion he had written of the evolution of the area from seabed teeming with marine life to a barren, glacier-covered mass. He had traced the settlement of the land following the melting of the ice by the Adena, Hopewell and Erie peoples, among others, and finally by the hardy pioneers who had created the town and a small college dedicated to music, the arts, and science.

From his studies, Sherman had concluded that: "The earth itself has a life like ours, though it grows young while growing old. Each day dawns with the face of a child, for dawn itself is ever present at the turning interface of time. The breezes stirring in the white pine above, the waters flowing below, the rising mists and falling rain, and all the motions of a million living things derive from a steady, central sun; yet always the energizing rays fall on a changing, creative scene."

"Tack this up on your wall, my good friend," said Hawley Short to Dwight Moodey, and contemplate the biologist's line: 'Each day dawns with the face of a child, for dawn itself is ever present at the turning interface of time.'

"That's really all that's important for us to know, how to grow younger while growing older, awakening each morning with a smile on our face, confident that this is what our little world is doing, too."

THE END